Collinson House

Collinson House

The View from the Dome

By Julie Blackburn

Foreword by Jim Mellon

This first edition first published in 2020
© 2020 Fruitful Publications Limited

Fruitful Publications Limited (t/a Fruitful Publications),
English company number 09314658.

Collinson House: The View from the Dome is a collection of reminiscences, facts and stories gathered by the authors to record the history of this unique property. It is not complete but rather a work in progress. If you would like to add any facts, photos or reflections you or your family may have, please contact **orders@fruitfulpublications.com**

Reproduced text and images in this book belong to Jim Mellon; his friends; local residents and their heirs; and Isle of Man collectors, websites, and museums. A list of those approached for permission is included in the author's note.

Additional images: p.71: ANL/Shutterstock; p80: By Gregory J Kingsley - Own work, CC BY-SA 3.0, https://commons.wikimedia.org

Every effort has been made to obtain the necessary permissions with reference to copyright material, both illustrative and quoted. We apologise for any omissions in this respect and will be pleased to make appropriate acknowledgement in any future editions.

A catalogue record of this book is available from the British Library.

ISBN: 978-0-99304-788-6

Book Design: Eliana Thompson

Printed by: Micropress Printers Ltd., Reydon, Suffolk, IP18 6SZ

Contents

Acknowledgements

We would like to thank the following people whose help in writing and producing this book was invaluable:

- Kate Firth and David Lythgoe for their enthusiasm and for sharing their family photos.

- Peter Fisher, for generously allowing us access to his wonderful photo archive.

- Manx National Heritage Museum, for their amazing archive of Isle of Man photographs and newspapers and especially Jude Dicken for all her help.

- Yvonne Cresswell, Curator of Social History, Manx National Heritage.

- Isle of Man Post Office for allowing us to use their beautiful images.

- Professor Hugh Davidson and all at Rushen Heritage Trust for their generous help.

- Imperial War Museum, London, for their remarkable archive of audio recordings with wartime internees.

- Jon Wornham for allowing us to use some of his beautiful images.

- Lincoln Forrest and Ben Humbles for their photos of the recent renovations.

And to those who shared their happy memories of Collinson House:

David Lythgoe, Keith McArd, Kate Firth, Sheila Bailey, Mandy Karsa, Phil Colebourn, Jennifer Quayle, Bryan Fullerton and others mentioned in the book.

The Hearts of Ellan stamps designed by Adam Berry for The Isle of Man Post Office.

Rear view of Collinson House.
Courtesy of Patricia Tutt.

Front view of Collinson House.
Courtesy of Patricia Tutt.

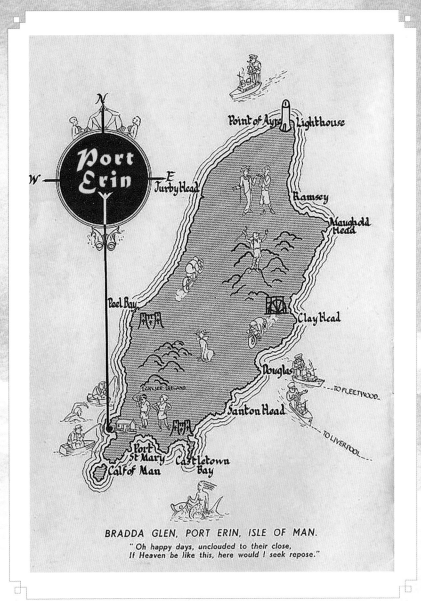

BRADDA GLEN, PORT ERIN, ISLE OF MAN.

*"Oh happy days, unclouded to their close,
If Heaven be like this, here would I seek repose."*

Author's Note

The Isle of Man is not part of the United Kingdom: like Jersey and Guernsey it is a self-governing British Crown Dependency.

It is one of the world's oldest democracies with a parliament, called Tynwald, that was established over 1,000 years ago. The Isle of Man equivalent of Members of Parliament in the UK are called Members of the House of Keys, or MHKs.

The island produces its own coins and banknotes, has its own language, Manx Gaelic, and many of its own everyday terms. For example, this story often refers to the local area's 'Commissioners': the nearest equivalent in UK terms would be parish councillors.

Conquered and settled by the Vikings in the late 8th century, the island became part of the Norse Kingdom of Mann and the Isles, along with the Hebrides and the islands of the Firth of Clyde before coming under Scottish rule. It was later ruled by the Stanley family, the earls of Derby, who took the title of *Lords of Mann*. The Queen is now the Lord of Mann and her island representative is the Lieutenant Governor.

Its position in the middle of the Irish Sea once gave it strategic importance and there was significant investment in castles and other fortifications. Some of these, like the beautifully preserved Castle Rushen in Castletown, remain to this day.

More recently the island was used, in both World War I and World War II, to house enemy aliens who were interned as a perceived risk to the war effort. The women's camp, in Port Erin, plays a significant role in this story.

For many centuries the island's economy was made up of fishing and farming and it was not until the early 1900s that tourism began to play a major role. More recently, when the 1960s and 70s saw the rise of package holidays abroad, the island changed its tax regime to stimulate the economy.

It now has very successful financial and e-gaming sectors and is internationally recognised as a stable and well-regulated jurisdiction in which to hold assets.

You can find more information about the Isle of Man at **www.locate.im.**

Foreword

I spent over 100 days at Collinson House during the Covid-19 lockdown, the longest period I have spent since I bought it about 20 years ago. The stay was marvellous, reinforcing my fondness for the place and allowing me the time to appreciate this magnificent house's charms, as well as of those of the Port Erin neighbourhood.

Over the lockdown, we made friends with a menagerie of animals and creatures, including Marmaduke the Manx cat, Julius and Fatima, the beach's resident seagulls, Charles the crow, and Geronimo the fish – all of whom helped us to pass the long days looking out at the Irish Sea.

Collinson House was a dilapidated wreck when I bought it. It required a programme of extensive works, including the addition of another floor below the old sprung dance floor and the installation of all the mod cons. Today, Collinson has undergone another renovation and I am looking forward to returning to the sparkling old girl when travel becomes possible again.

Julie Blackburn is an old friend of mine and a very accomplished writer. She has researched and written a wonderful book about the history of this iconic building. The place looks unprepossessing from the street, but from Bradda Head it is impossible to mistake the splendid dome and the glass and stone edifice perched on the opposite cliff. Once inside, the sweeping circular windows afford stunning views of the beach and sea. Sometimes it is calm, but we can often hear the waves crashing onto the shore.

We also look out on the old mines hidden in the rocks below Bradda Head, and imagine the miners picking their way gingerly along the treacherous ledges.

I regard myself as a custodian of Collinson House and will work to continuously preserve and improve it, as a vital part of Port Erin's – and the Isle of Man's – heritage.

Jim Mellon
December 2020.

Marmaduke, the tailless Manx cat, during the recent works in the garden. *Courtesy of Dafina Grapci.*

Jim and Marmaduke.
Courtesy of Dafina Grapci.

Ted Collinson. *Courtesy of Kate Firth*

Chapter One

TED COLLINSON

Imagine:

it's the winter of 1912–13 and you're perched precariously on the side of a cliff where the westerly gales blowing in from the Irish Sea hit you with such force they take your breath away.

Mortar and stone are being lowered from the top in buckets and your hands are so cold you fumble to unload them. When the lads on the gantry above call down to you, their voices are whipped away on the wind or drowned out by the sound of the waves crashing onto the beach a hundred feet below you.

You're not even being paid much: labour is cheap these days.

You wonder how the grandiose structure proposed on the plans will ever be completed and you certainly don't imagine that it will still be clinging fiercely to the side of that cliff more than one hundred years later.

But it is. Collinson House remains right where you built it, a testament to the power of imagination and will over the dull and the everyday...

Looking North-West from Port Erin beach in 1911, before the construction of Collinson's. Note Milner's Tower in the distance.

A closer look at Milner's Tower.

It was in October 1912 that the people living in the seaside village of Port Erin on the Isle of Man first heard of an intriguing new development being proposed.

The *Isle of Man Times* carried a report on a meeting of the Port Erin Commissioners at which a planning application was discussed for 'a massive restaurant for Messrs Collinsons'.

The plans were passed and locals watched with increasing curiosity and awe as an extraordinary building began to take shape above the bay. This was looking like no other restaurant they had ever seen before.

It was hard to comprehend fully the scale and strangeness of it from the road that wound past its front entrance but if you took a walk around the headland, or up nearby Bradda hillside, you could see it in all its glory.

It was round for a start, and very large. It had an intricate roof of rosemary tiles, topped by a fanciful dome. At the back, a semi-circular wooden balcony looked out over the bay.

People living on the Isle of Man would have known the name of Collinson's as there were already two Collinson's Cafés in Douglas, the island's capital. The company was renowned for its tea and coffee blending and for sparing no expense on the opulent interior décor of their cafés, all rich velvets and fringing on the lampshades in the style of the day. So maybe it wasn't so surprising that they were setting out to build something special.

And it is with the Collinson family that the remarkable story of Collinson House really begins.

In 1835 a twenty-four year old Lancashire lad called Thomas Collinson came to live in Halifax and took over a shop there, in Cornmarket. It already boasted a large golden canister sign over the door so he called his new business 'The Golden Canister'.

It began as a licensed agency for the sale of stout and porter but that didn't sit well with Thomas, who was a devout Quaker: he decided that he should not be selling intoxicants and switched to tea and coffee instead.

'Black and green teas, refined sugar, spices and hops' are the products listed in his early advertisements. Thomas also travelled around the surrounding countryside in a dogcart selling his products. The firm prospered and from 1840 gradually expanded. It was just as well as Thomas and his wife, Mary, were thought to have had at least 10 children.

Cornflour and coffee were among the products sold by Collinson & Sons. *Courtesy of Calderdale Museums, Halifax.*

Two of his sons, Joseph and Edward, grew up and joined the business which became T. Collinson and Sons. They acquired a warehouse which was used for tea and coffee blending and opened a shop and café, in Brighouse, followed by others in Bradford, Huddersfield, Blackpool, Bolton and Buxton.

By the time Thomas died in 1885 he was a highly respected local alderman, despite also being rather eccentric. Apparently, he had a great aversion to banks and would hide his money all around his premises.

His grandson, Edward Whiteley Collinson, who was born in 1879, also joined the business and in 1896 it became a limited company. We may imagine that we invented the coffee house culture but it has actually been around since the 17th century and it was certainly alive and flourishing in the early part of the 20th century.

And, by this time, the Collinson's Café chain would have been the approximate equivalent of a Costa or a Starbucks except that all their cafés also had a counter selling their specially blended coffee and loose leaf teas. People commented on the wonderful aroma when they went into the cafés.

As a young man with an eye to continuing and building on the success of the business, Edward Collinson, or 'Ted' as he was known in the family, must have considered an expansion into the Isle of Man an obvious move.

Even just fifty years earlier, life on this small island in the middle of the Irish Sea had been a struggle for many of its people. They eked out a living from farming small crofts and fishing and their diet was typically 'spuds 'n herring'. Significant numbers of Manx people had fled the grinding poverty to try their luck in America or, later, Australia.

But things were changing as tourism started to transform the fortunes of the island.

In 1830, the introduction of a steam ship passenger service between Liverpool and Douglas signalled the start of large numbers of visitors coming to the Isle of Man. On June 30th the Isle of Man Steam Packet Company's vessel, *Mona's Isle*, newly-built at a cost of £7,250, set out from Douglas to Liverpool on its inaugural voyage.

By 1912, the company was operating 14 passenger steamers and a cargo vessel, ferrying more than half a million visitors to the island every year between late May and the end of September. As well as Liverpool they were also operating ferry services to and from Ardrossan, Belfast, Dublin, Whitehaven and Fleetwood and day excursions to Warrenpoint, Llandudno and Stranraer.

The Isle of Man is 32 miles long and 13 miles wide – not large but still more than four times the size of Jersey so there are plenty of wide open spaces where you can walk, in the hills or along the 100 miles of coastal footpaths.

Ted Collinson as a young man.
Courtesy of Kate Firth.

A report in *The Spectator* in 1880 was rather sniffy about the 'mostly lower middle class' visitors that the island attracted. However, it went on to say: 'But the Isle of Man may fairly claim a visit from persons of higher culture than these. Regarded simply as a health resort, there can be no question that it is the most thorough sea residence in the kingdom.'

Yvonne Cresswell, Curator of Social History at Manx National Heritage, makes the point that, in those days, the Isle of Man was like going abroad for many people, with all the advantages of going abroad but none of the disadvantages such as different languages and currency.

However, there were some differences in the way things were done on the Island and they did not always go down well, as Yvonne goes on to explain: 'In British hotels and boarding houses you'd have a system of separate tables: if you were in a party of one, you sat at a table for one person. On the Isle of Man they worked it by the continental style of everybody sitting round the table together.'

'This had the advantage that you could come off the boat first thing in the morning, go to your boarding house and after your first meal you'd met people, chatted and maybe got friends you could go round the island with.

'For a lot of people in strait-laced Britain, that wasn't a good idea.'

But this, she adds, led to the Isle of Man becoming a favourite with the younger, less formal generation of Brits, very often looking for romance: 'The Isle of Man was quite "18–30"!'

Although many Scottish people visited the island, by far the largest numbers of holidaymakers came from the north of England and they would already have been familiar with the Collinson's brand. And all these considerations must have weighed in the decision to open a Collinson's Café on the Isle of Man in Douglas.

In 1905, an advert running in the Isle of Man press proclaimed: 'For Pure Tea, Collinson's. For Finest Coffee In The World, Collinson's.'

Another café was opened in Douglas, followed later by an ice factory. And then Ted Collinson turned his attention to Port Erin.

Formerly a small fishing port, Port Erin, along with its neighbour Port St Mary, is situated on a peninsula in the southwest of the island, in the parish of Rushen. Tourism had arrived there in the 1880s with the opening of the Isle of Man Steam Railway, which still runs today. Its route is along a narrow-gauge track from Douglas via Castletown and Port St Mary, terminating in Port Erin, the same one that would have carried holidaymakers in those far-off days.

Postcard of haystacks in Port Erin, circa 1900.

As a newly discovered tourist destination, Port Erin had a lot going for it. Winters may be harsh but, in the summertime, it is a delight. Its bay looks westwards across the Irish Sea and, on any reasonably clear day, you can see the mountains of Mourne. Stunning sunsets frequently paint the evening sky in bold reds and oranges.

Port Erin also has, in the opinion of many – although the people of Peel might give you an argument on this – the best beach on the island.

The 1913 Isle of Man Steam Packet guidebook described it thus: 'Port Erin has sprung to prominence during the last decade or so as being one of the most desirable localities for the visitor in search of health and recreation... As a bathing place Port Erin is unrivalled in the Isle of Man. Beside the beautiful sandy beach there is an artificial bath built for mixed bathing under the shelter of the cliffs, which is much patronised.'

The bustling Promenade at Port Erin. *Courtesy of Peter Fisher.*

Permitting 'mixed bathing' in what we would now of course call a 'swimming pool', was most unusual, and probably a little daring, when the Traie Meanagh (Middle Bay) baths opened in 1899. The open-air swimming baths in Douglas, opened in 1874, had been 'for gentlemen only'. These gentlemen had swum naked and old photos of the time clearly show rows of women on the headland above, watching them.

According to a Port Erin Commissioners' guide book the Traie Meanagh baths featured: 'One of Tangye's Engines, supplying 520 gallons of sea water per minute, to ensure fresh water daily' in the pool.' Rows of wooden seating were erected on the cliffs above it and became an enormously popular viewing spot for the diving contests that took place.

Scandalous! Men and women bathe together in Port Erin.
Courtesy of Peter Fisher

Port Erin beach was overlooked by a promenade of stately Victorian terraced buildings, most of which were boarding houses or hotels. But it was not here that Ted Collinson had chosen to build his new café. His location was above the village and just around the headland from the swimming pool, on what was possibly the most stunning site on the whole island.

Perched on the side of a cliff overlooking the sea, as one brochure later noted: 'It commands one of the finest sea views in the British Isles'.

Ted purchased the site in June 1912 from a certain Mrs Florence Holford Laughton, widow of the High Bailiff of Peel, Alfred Nelson Laughton, who had died the previous year. Mrs Laughton had been one of the founders of the Manx cultural institution known to one and all as 'The Guild', an annual competition covering a long list of singing and dancing classes that still takes place on the island.

The original title deeds from 1912.

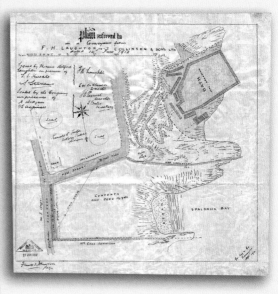

A plan of the land sold by Mrs Laughton.

The site she sold to Collinson's also included ownership of the foreshore below, a small pebble beach known as Spaldrick Bay. The conveyance includes a covenant limiting the activity on the beach to 'rowing boats and twelve or less number of bathing vans or tents'. You might construe this as Mrs Laughton taking a dim view of the new fashion for sea bathing but it could be more likely that she wanted to protect the business at the nearby Traie Meanagh swimming baths which she also owned at the time.

Next door to the site was Bradda, a hillside promontory with a pretty glen at its base. At the top of the hill stands Milner's Tower, a curious stone structure built in the shape of a lock to honour one of the village's benefactors who had been a safe-maker.

It was from the top of this hill that a photograph of the view over the sea in the direction of the Calf of Man, a nearby islet, was taken in 1931. This image famously won Kodak's first World Photographic Contest and Collinson's shared this view.

The prize-winning photo from Bradda Head. © Manx National Heritage (PG/6636)

However, stunning as it was, it was not going to be an easy site to build on, especially not the structure that Ted was planning.

COLLINSON'S CAFÉ
PORT ERIN
ISLE OF MAN

Chapter Two

CONSTRUCTION

The firm of architects commissioned by Ted Collinson to design his new café was Clement Williams & Sons of Halifax and there were several good reasons for this choice.

The firm was one of the best known in Halifax: they had been responsible for some of its major buildings, including the Alexandra Hall and Victoria Theatre, and they had already carried out work for the Collinson family.

More importantly, the principal, William Clement Williams FRIBA, was a regular visitor to Port Erin and had become so fond of the place he had had a house built there, Beacon Croft. He may even have been the one who found the site for Ted Collinson and spotted its potential.

What he envisaged was, to say the least, ambitious. This was not to be just any old seaside café.

The Villa Marina Kursaal, on Douglas promenade, was also completed in 1913. It had previously been the residence of the Lieutenant Governor of the island. The addition of a large extension with a distinctive domed roof had converted it into an entertainment complex. It has been suggested that this design might have influenced the design of Collinson House.

The Villa Marina Kursaal in Douglas, from a contemporary postcard.

Collinson's has also been described, less flatteringly, as 'an architectural mix of Asiatic, late Gothic and Ealing Broadway'. But Professor Ian Davidson, chairman of Rushen Heritage Trust, says: 'I think the building is very successful. It has impact, a strong personality, is very distinctive, occupies a commanding site and has become a long-standing landmark.'

In November 1912, the *Isle of Man Examiner* revealed that McArd's had been chosen to build the new café, at an estimated cost of £3,000.

This would have been no surprise: the McArds had already built a good many of the houses and hotels in Port Erin. The firm was set up in the 1850s and ran for 160 years, through five generations of the McArd family.

Keith McArd, now in his eighties, remembers hearing about how his grandfather, Joseph, and father, John Joseph, worked on the site.

He said: 'Oh it was a difficult site in those days: there was no machinery, there were no big cranes even, or anything. Everything had to be hand humped and handled and [Collinson House] was all built in local stone: they weren't importing stone in those days.

'But labour was cheap then.'

Many of the things we now take for granted on construction sites simply did not exist back then. For example, the first-ever delivery of ready mixed concrete in the world did not take place until the following year.

Keith recalled: 'They must have hand mixed all the concrete. My dad had a big framework on the yard with a mesh in it and the men used to have to throw the sand up through that to get all the muck out of it. It went through the mesh and landed on the other side and it was nice clean sand...I don't know how they would have got it down [from the top of the hill] other than by setting up a gantry and pulley with two men on either side, lowering buckets.'

BY THEIR DEEDS
MR. JOHN JOSEPH McARD

John Joseph McArd became a prominent figure in the development of Port Erin. *The Isle of Man Times* depicted him in cartoon form years later, in 1935.

Aerial view of the Collinson site – note the steep gradient on which the house is built.
Courtesy of Jon Wornham.

Astonishingly, despite all the difficulties posed by the site and the complicated nature of the building's design, by the spring of 1913 it was already nearing completion.

On June 3rd that year, William Clement Williams died. The *Manx Quarterly* later reported:

'Mr Williams passed away at Beacon Croft, Port Erin, in his 67th year, and the news came as a shock to his numerous friends, by whom he was greatly esteemed, his charming personality having gained for him the warmest admiration. Mr Williams was naturally of a retiring disposition, and took no part in public affairs. His whole heart was in his profession, and some of the most important buildings in Halifax were designed by him. Many churches, chapels, schools, and factories are the expression of his genius.'

COLLINSON'S CAFÉ

Is one of the chief attractions of the Southern part of the Island. Perched on the cliff edge, with its own grounds stretching right down to the beach, it commands one of the finest sea views in the British Isles.

LUNCH.   SNACKS.   AFTERNOON TEA.   ICES, Etc.

Accomodation for 300.   Balcony and Verandah.   Bathing Tents for Hire.

SPALDRICK,   PORT   ERIN.

An advertisement for Collinson's Café in the *Isle of Man Times* from September 1913 – only a few months after opening.

Later that month, on June 28th, the *Isle of Man Examiner* was eagerly anticipating the imminent opening of the new café:

'Messrs Collinson's new café at Spaldrick, Port Erin, when it is opened for the season, will doubtless prove a great attraction to visitors. Seated on the balcony, where refreshments are provided, one may obtain an excellent view of the panorama of Port Erin Bay, Bradda Head and on to the Calf. The surrounding country, too, which at this time of the year is so beautiful, may be seen to advantage from the café.

'The chalet is built in a pretty style of architecture, and a dome ornaments the tea rooms. Almost from the basement of the café the cliffs run down to the sea.'

Collinson's Café perched on the clifftop. *Courtesy of Peter Fisher.*

An early view of the front of the Café from the road. *Courtesy of Peter Fisher.*

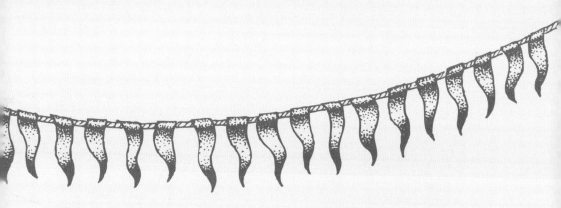

The actual opening date is unknown but there are photographs of how the café entrance, on the road that runs along the top of the cliff, would have looked. There were two bay windows on either side of the door and a sign reading 'Collinson's Café' placed above it at a jaunty angle.

Despite this sign, for some unknown reason, the café continued to be referred to as 'Spaldrick bungalow' or the 'Spaldrick café' for many years, even in Collinson's own applications for music and drinks licences.

Its opening would have taken place against the backdrop of a tourism success story that looked as though it would never end. In 1913 the weather was reported to have been 'exceptionally fine throughout the season' and the Isle of Man recorded its highest ever visitor numbers, 663,000. Black and white film footage of the day shows a moving mass of people, almost without a break, along Douglas's main streets and promenade. And whilst the majority of visitors were accommodated in Douglas, Port Erin would have had its fair share, both of people staying in the village and those coming down for the day on the steam railway.

Collinson's Café advert from December 1919.
Courtesy of Isle of Man Times.

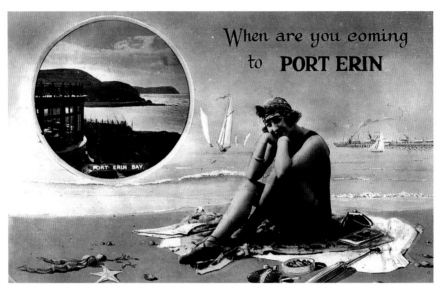

When are you coming to **PORT ERIN**

PORT ERIN BAY.

A view of Collinson's Café overlooking Port Erin Bay (inset) from a contemporary tourism advertisement.

The idea that war might break out the following year seems to have occurred to no one. Or, if it did, given the history of previous wars, they had no concept of a 'world war'. They probably thought that life would more or less carry on as normal and had no inkling of what was coming their way. Any other mindset would have made an investment in a 'massive new restaurant' seem very foolhardy.

And, whatever storm clouds may have been gathering on the horizon, in February 1914 the Isle of Man Steam Packet Company's Director's Report remained smugly complacent as they described a 'record year' and a six per cent dividend.

Their new, geared-turbine steamer, *King Orry*, capable of carrying 2,550 passengers, had been brought into service: 'During the time she was in commission the vessel fully maintained the speed contracted for and was very popular with the travelling public'.

In March 1914 Collinson's were applying to the Castletown Licensing Court for a music licence for their newest café, saying 'we require a licence only for instrumental music: there will be no singing'. A licence was granted, to run each day from 10am–11pm.

On June 28th, there came news of the assassination of Archduke Franz Ferdinand. Despite this, a few weeks later, on Saturday July 18th, the *Isle of Man Examiner* was more concerned with the fact that the Steam Packet Company had made 'ample preparations to cope with the invasion' caused by 'The Scotch Fair Week – or in other words, the annual holidays for Glasgow and district' which commenced that week-end. It listed all the sailings planned by the operator's ships including *Mona's Queen*, *Ben-my-Chree* and the much-lauded *King Orry*.

Ten days later, on July 28th, World War One began.

Stamps commemorating the Manx contribution to the Allied effort in the First World War. *Courtesy of the Isle of Man Post Office.*

BRADDA HEAD, PORT ERIN, I.O.M.

Sunset at Collinson's Café. *Courtesy of Peter Fisher.*

Chapter Three

War and its Aftermath

The war had an immediate effect on tourism with the number of passengers carried by the Isle of Man Steam Packet Company in 1914 down by more than 340,000 on the previous record year.

Their shareholders' report stated: 'The directors regret that the year's trading and profits show a large reduction owing to the effect of the war, which broke out just at what is generally the company's busiest period.'

Four of the company's steamers were requisitioned by the British Government in October and November 1914, and four more in 1915.

This decimated what had previously been described as 'the greatest and most renowned fleet that ever existed'.

One newspaper editorial commented that: 'That fleet, having the greatest horsepower in proportion to tonnage of any fleet, deep sea or otherwise... was by far the most useful fleet for a British Government at war. A nation, not represented in the British Parliament and not able to dictate a word on its own behalf, loyally handed over their remarkable boats.'

The Ramsey during its civilian service.

In August 1915 one of the vessels, *The Ramsey*, went down whilst on Government service in the North Sea with many lives lost.

As for the other requisitioned vessels, according to the chairman of the Steam Packet: 'for the most part, we do not know where they are, or what work they are engaged in, but we must all trust and hope they are rendering good service to our King and his Empire.'

By 1916 tourism was virtually non-existent, with visitors deterred by the lack of boats available to transport them and also by the very real threat of German submarines lurking in the Irish Sea. In the worst years of the war passenger numbers dropped to around 70,000.

It seems fair to assume that Collinson's Café in Port Erin, which in any case only opened for the summer season, would have been closed, probably from the end of the 1914 season until the war was over.

But 1918 saw the recovery begin. In October of that year it was reported that 'over 90 per cent more passengers have travelled – a very remarkable increase'.

As one commentator writing in the *Isle of Man Examiner* in October 1918 put it: 'During the period 1916–17 almost every kind of excuse was made for not visiting the Isle of Man – from fear of submarines downwards – but now... twice as many cheerfully exercised the greatest patience to get to the island anyhow, and twice as many more would have clamoured to go had more steamers been able to run.

'For three years there have been a host of Manx pessimists who dolefully declared that it would take five years for the island to "recover", now they see that it will take much nearer five minutes.'

A banner for Knockaloe internment camp.
Courtesy of the Mannin Collections Archive.

That optimism was slightly misplaced as 1918–19 saw the world once more turned upside down by the Spanish Flu, a pandemic that killed 50 million people across the globe, and the Isle of Man was not immune.

In January 1919, an outbreak on the island was widely reported in the press. It was believed to have originated when 200 prisoners of war were transferred from an internment camp in England to Knockaloe camp, on the west of the island. The guards who came with them had previously been at the front and there was speculation that they had carried the infection with them from France.

Joseph Pilates, the German exercise pioneer, at Knockaloe internment camp.
© *Manx National Heritage (PG/7870/38822).*

Advice to Sufferers.

The attention of our readers is drawn to the Government notice re the influenza epidemic, and the public are asked to follow the instructions, especially those as to the avoidance of crowded places, and those as to what to do in case of an attack.

There is no very serious risk to life if people exercise due precautions. In simple, uncomplicated cases, convalescence supervenes in the course of a week or so; but influenza is very frequently conjoined with bronchitis or pneumonia, in which case it is much more persistent and dangerous. There is, moreover, an extreme proneness to relapse on the slightest exposure, even after the patient feels perfectly recovered. The greatest danger is from people trying to fight the disease down, instead of taking to their beds and nursing the attack.

The following instructions have been issued by the Imperial Local Government Board:—

Avoid scattering infection by sneezing and coughing.

Boil ...

Exp...

Owing to the number of deaths occurring as the result of Influenza, His Excellency the Lieutenant-Governor has issued a Proclamation (a copy of which is appended), under the Local Government Board Consolidation Act, 1916, embodying certain regulations made by the Local Government Board with a view to preventing and guarding against the spread of the disease.

Any person who wilfully violates any of the said regulations is liable to a penalty not exceeding twenty pounds.

The general public is requested to co-operate with the authorities in preventing the spread of the epidemic.

The following instructions should be carefully observed by members of the general public:—

1. Avoid crowded places, especially dances, parties, and similar forms of amusement.
2. Keep doors and windows open, and sleep in well-ventilated bedrooms.
3. Brush teeth frequently, and use antiseptic gargles.
4. If headache, shivering, or joint pains are felt, go to bed immediately, and consult a doctor.
5. Strict isolation should be enforced in every affected case.

By Order,

B. E. SARGEAUNT,
Government Secretary.
Government Office. Isle of Man,
11th January, 1919.

GOVERNMENT NOTICES (continued).

INFLUENZA EPIDEMIC IN PEEL DISTRICT.

MODIFICATION OF RESTRICTIONS.

THE Lieutenant-Governor has issued a Proclamation dated 7th March, 1919, a copy of which is appended, embodying new Regulations made by the Local Government Board in connection with the outbreak of Influenza in the Peel District.

The Proclamation permits Churches, Chapels, and other Places of Worship to re-open after being properly cleansed and disinfected.

By Order,

Advice from the *Isle of Man Times* from January 1919 on measures to combat the Spanish Flu.

In a move all too recognisable during the more recent Covid-19 pandemic, schools were closed and pupils sent home and restrictions were placed on cinemas, theatres and dances. Workshops, factories, railway carriages and 'public conveyances' were required to be disinfected daily.

By early February fifty people on the island had died but there were signs that the epidemic was beginning to fade away.

A populace more than ready for some fun and cheer in their lives was increasingly looking to dancing to lift their post-war spirits. And this was about to have a major impact on Collinson House.

In the early 1900s the popularity of the waltz had been challenged by the introduction of the foxtrot from America. Just before the war, the Argentine tango was being performed in Paris and was gaining respectability: in 1914, Queen Mary herself had requested a tango demonstration.

The war had played a big part in breaking down ideas of what was and was not 'proper' for women in relation to many aspects of life. More than 100,000 women had joined the armed forces during the war and many others had stepped up to take over the jobs of men who were called away to fight. This was a generation who were not about to be told the sort of dancing they should be doing.

It was all about the music, too. By the end of the war, rag music and jazz had arrived from America and their syncopated rhythms were inspiring a whole new genre of dance.

In 1919 the Hammersmith Palais de Danse opened its doors, one of many dance halls starting up around the country. As the public demand for dance venues grew, all the best hotels, as well as dance halls in Britain's top seaside resorts, started holding tea dances.

The Isle of Man wasn't slow to catch on.

The Whitsun weekend of 1919 signalled the official start to the first summer season after the war. *Mona's Herald* on June 4th 1919 reported on the reopening of the Palace ballroom in Douglas: 'It will be the first time since the commencement of the war that this lovely pleasure house will be available to the seeker after innocent recreation.

'Until recently the Palace ballroom was utilized in the grim task of facilitating the end of the war. On Saturday next, it will once more be a picture of pleasure at its finest, and some special features will be introduced to mark the occasion.'

The following week, the same reporter commented: 'The vogue for dancing is so universal and so catholic in its appeal that one wonders how visitors could enjoy Douglas when the Palace ballroom, with its perfect floor and Mr Barry Wood's fine orchestra, was "verboten".'

The Palace ballroom was the centre of Douglas' cultural life.
Courtesy of Manx National Heritage (M 22762/1)

Yvonne Cresswell, Curator of Social History at Manx National Heritage, said: 'I don't think we have any idea just how important dancing was then.

'I always get the impression that, because there were so many dance halls on the island, you could literally leave your hotel first thing in the morning after breakfast and dance your way round the island and come back at maybe three o'clock in the morning.'

The Manx newspapers even had their own correspondent for dancing: 'Jazz', writing in the *Isle of Man Examiner* in 1922, posed the question: 'Have you ever thought that the girl who works through an ordinary ballroom programme must have got over the ground to the tune of thirty miles or so?'

The dance craze had also been spotted by Ted Collinson, who obviously kept a keen eye out for new ways to attract people to his cafés.

In 1920, he founded a brand new company, Beech's Fine Chocolates in Preston, which is still going today. It seems likely that chocolates, and ice cream from their 'ice factory' in Douglas, would now have been sold in all the Collinson's cafés and shops, alongside their loose leaf teas and ground coffees. It would be fair to say, in modern terms, that Ted was aiming to position Collinson's as a premium brand.

And so, addressing the dance craze, Ted turned his attentions to the Port Erin café and, once again, his plans were ambitious and the investment generous. The café had been granted a 'music and dancing' licence in 1920 but there was limited space for this, so Ted decided to embark upon a major expansion and refurbishment.

A postcard showing the new and improved Collinson's Café, after the extension.

In December 1921 plans were passed to extend the balcony of Collinson House by 'putting out a veranda', for people to occupy. Photographs taken at the time show the veranda, built below the original wooden balcony and considerably larger. This took the structure even further out over the cliff and stone buttresses at its base were needed to reinforce it.

To accommodate a ballroom, the veranda was then enclosed by a semi-circular wall of windows, looking out to sea. The wooden balcony above was enlarged too, covering the whole of the ballroom roof.

It is not clear at exactly what point the 'extended balcony' noted in the planning application was altered to form the enclosed ballroom, and it appears from later reports that planning was never specifically granted for this.

This discrepancy was later to cause much argument and discussion in Port Erin Commissioners' meetings as no one had apparently noticed at the time that one corner of the new veranda had been erected over the main sewer.

It was reported that 'no member of the then Board ever thought that a dancing pavilion was going to be erected, but advantage had been taken of that to put up the present ballroom.'

Despite the grumbling Ted had got away with it. At a time when tourism was the be-all and end-all of the economy on the Isle of Man, it was hardly likely that any authority would have taken serious steps against someone who had provided such a splendid facility for their area.

And 'splendid' is undoubtedly the word for the ballroom that Collinson's Café now boasted. They had set out to construct not just any old ballroom but 'the finest dancefloor in Europe'. The McArds once again carried out the work and no expense had been spared on it, using the finest Canadian maple.

It was also 'sprung' to absorb shock and give a softer feeling, as Keith McArd explained: 'Beneath the floor there were joists running and then there were the springs sitting on them. Then there were more joists going the other way, underneath the floor boards, to sit on top of the springs.

'The heaviest joists were the ones underneath the springs, the others were just to even the load of the springs onto the floorboards. The springs were big, about six inches, and there were a lot of them.'

More than 70 years later, when Keith himself was asked to carry out some building works on Collinson House that involved digging out under the dancefloor, he discovered 'the original grease was still on the springs: they were immaculate'.

It was time for the dancing to begin...

Dance at Collinson's Cafe.

Winter time, in the Isle of Man, might aptly be termed the season of our discontent, because the Island, with its unparalleled scenery, and exquisitely beautiful surroundings, together with its many forms of amusement in the summer time, is indeed an enviable abode, but when autumn is past, and winter takes her place, accompanied by sleet, rain, and snow, the Island becomes dark, dreary, and dismal. It is all the more refreshing, therefore, to discover that there are a few people at least in our midst who are eager and willing to take the initiative in giving pleasure to their young friends and acquaintances; and what more innocent pleasure is it possible to find than that of a private subscription dance? On Tuesday we commemorated the most momentous day in the history of the British Empire, we celebrated the anniversary of the downfall of Prussianism; and, with this in mind, four of the best known Douglas gentlemen determined, as a celebration of this event, to give a dance at Collinson's Cafe. The gentlemen in question are four demobilised officers—Messrs R. D. Farrant, F. W. Smith-Cleburne, H. Cowin, and V. Brearey. The idea "caught on"—if one might be permitted a common expression —tremendously, and the dance took place yesterday evening. Perhaps it is almost unnecessary to state here that it was an unqualified success. The dancing floor at Collinson's has not its equal in the Island, and is universally known; and the large room, with its brightly polished floor and its myriads of Japanese lanterns, certainly presented a most attractive appearance. Just a little time before eight o'clock, the guests, of whom there must have been well nigh fifty, commenced streaming in in couples and threes. The frocks of the ladies contrasted vividly with the more sombre coloured gentlemen's evening dress, and just added the necessary amount of colour to the scene. Mr Bing's orchestra discoursed the latest dance music, and the couples danced to their hearts' content until the last strain had died away. The dance programme was varied, from the waltz to the ubiquitous Jazz, and so catered for all tastes. The danger of every dance given is the fear that at some time or other during the evening there is liable to be a drag of time; but, under the guidance of these four gentlemen, nothing of this description happened. Everyone, apparently, was out for enjoyment, and to throw themselves heart and soul of the task of making others enjoy themselves. Perhaps the day they were celebrating had something to do with it, but, at all events, the result was highly gratifying. The ladies wore, well, just

To celebrate the anniversary of the Armistice (or the "downfall of Prussianism", as this article calls it), a dance was held at Collinson's with fifty young people in attendance. From the *Isle of Man Times*, November 1919.

Chapter Four

COMPETITION ARRIVES

A transaction had taken place in 1920 which would definitely have caught the eye of Ted Collinson: a property known as 'The Hut', along with its grounds, was purchased by one George Lucas Trustrum.

What we now know as the beautiful Bradda Glen, adjacent to Collinson House, had long been in private ownership. During the mid-1800s Mr A. W. Adams, the Isle of Man's Clerk of the Rolls, had built The Hut there, as a summer residence.

The rather unflattering name did not reflect what old photos show to have been a pretty building with a thatched roof. It had a sitting-room, two bedrooms, kitchens, and a servants' room. Outside there was a greenhouse, a boathouse, and a bathing-house.

Mr Adams died in 1883, and on August 7th of that year The Hut was put up for auction. The advertisement for the auction included the following description: 'Its position is one of the most charming in the United Kingdom commanding a magnificent stretch of sea coast.

'It is enclosed in its own grounds, which extend for a half-mile along the Bay. A large portion of the land is laid out with choice Shrubs, Evergreens, and other Trees. Another portion is arranged as a Rabbit Warren, and walled in on the land side, and contains an abundance of rabbits. Fishing and Shooting can be enjoyed without leaving the grounds. In a cove underneath the grounds there is ample shelter for a yacht. In fact, a more perfect marine residence could not be found.'

It was bought by Mr Isaac Thorpe, a resident of Manchester. The *Isle of Man Examiner* reported that Mr Thorpe 'owns the yacht Hermit, which at present lies in Port Erin bay, and he has been a visitor to the Island for some years.'

In March 1892 readers of the same newspaper were informed that 'Mr Charles Jennison, County Councillor of Lancashire, owner of the Belle Vue Zoological Gardens, Manchester, and a frequent visitor to Port Erin, has purchased The Hut with the intention of residing there during the summer months.

On June 13th 1896 there had been drama when The Hut caught fire. According to the *Examiner*: 'The fire broke out at ten minutes past two o'clock this afternoon. There was not much wind, and the sparks falling on the thatched roof quickly set up a blaze which was seen from the Promenade.

'Scores of visitors and residents hurried to The Hut, and began to throw upon the burning roof what water was available on the premises, but the supply ran short, and then a chain of willing helpers was formed, and they passed buckets of water up from the bay itself.

'At half-past three the fire was got under control, but not until the servants' department had been practically destroyed. The furniture was all saved by the efforts of the people present. Mr Jennison is away, and it is not known whether the house and furniture are insured.'

In 1914 Mr Jennison died and The Hut is presumed to have lain empty during the war years but in March 1920 its future changed with the Trustrum purchase. George Trustrum, who had been Jennison's agent, came from a well-known Port Erin family and was said to already 'own half the town', including York House, The Eagle Hotel and the Falcon's Nest.

Trustrum planned to convert The Hut into a café and he must have moved quickly because in June 1920 he was granted a six-day licence for music and dancing.

A newspaper article on July 31st described the new venue in glowing terms: 'An additional attraction has been provided for residents in Port Erin and visitors there to, in the opening to the public of the beautiful grounds of "The Hut", situated on the northern edge of the bay.

'Now Mr G.L.Trustrum has purchased it, and he has given general admission to it on payment of a small charge. The approach is by a footpath from the main road to Bradda, through an avenue of shrubbery, in itself quite a beautiful walk.

'In the front of the residence is an open terrace, and this is being utilised as an open-air refreshment space. On a fine day one cannot imagine a lovelier place. The Calf Island and the Castle Rocks are in front, and very frequently the Irish mountains are seen in the distance.

'The principal use of the interior of "The Hut" is that of a small café. Mr Trustrum has built a small hall at the outer end of the Hut and this will be used by concert parties and other entertainers.'

The Hut and Grounds, Port Erin, I.O.M.

Tourists and locals alike made use of The Hut and its grounds. *Courtesy of Peter Fisher.*

The Hut appears to have been an instant success. In September it was reported that: 'The last few weeks of beautiful weather have been very beneficial to the attendance at The Hut, Port Erin.

'Every afternoon between 1,500 and 2,000 persons have passed the gate to enjoy the scenery and partake of tea in the grounds, and Mr Trustrum's staff have been very busy.'

One can imagine Ted Collinson looking down from his café, watching these hordes of people trooping into a rival venue, right under his nose, and being not at all pleased.

A view of Port Erin from The Hut grounds. Note Collinson's Café on the left: Ted would have seen his popular rival every time he glanced out of the window. *Courtesy of Peter Fisher.*

The competition was definitely on.

Ted's company had been trading on the Isle of Man, as in England, as T. Collinson & Sons Limited but in 1921 a new company was formed, Collinson's (IOM), with 9,300 shares at £1 and Ted as its chairman. This would consolidate his base on the Isle of Man and allow him to move forward, as we have already seen, with the plans to extend the Port Erin café and put in place the ballroom.

As well as tapping into the dance craze at the time it might also have been a move designed to see off the competition from Trustrum.

However, the fact that he had apparently got away with enclosing the veranda and constructing the dance floor had not made him popular with some of the local bigwigs and when, in 1924, he decided to extend the café even further, he hit a snag.

In November of that year, plans were being discussed by the Commissioners for 'an addition to Collinson's Café, on the headland overlooking Spaldrick creek.'

Naturally this brought up once more the matter of the veranda being over the sewer which had already caused so much consternation and discussion. The simmering resentment harboured by a few of the commissioners towards Collinson's, believing that the company had pulled a fast one on them with the ballroom, was now given a chance to air itself.

The veranda of Collinson's at sunset. *Courtesy of Peter Fisher.*

AT PORT ERIN.

Mr Jefferson's talented little orchestra at Collinson's Cafe, Port Erin, concludes its season's engagement to-morrow night (Saturday). The orchestra, consisting of Mr Jefferson, piano; Miss Edwardes, violin; Mr Lloyd, banjo; and Mrs B. Humphries, drums; has made a name for itself in the South this summer, and many hundreds of visitors to the Cafe have expressed their delight with the dance music provided. Mr Lloyd, the banjoist, will play with the Syncopated Six at the Villa next week.

Live music was an important part of the Collinson's brand. The resident orchestra in 1923 was particularly popular, as this notice from the *Isle of Man Examiner* makes clear.

Apparently 'a very long discussion took place' over the plans for a further addition to Collinson's Café in Port Erin. 'This matter has been discussed, off and on, for many months, and such versions of the proceedings as have obtained circulation have excited great interest among the general public...many years ago Collinson's built their café, and afterwards made an addition in the form of what has become their ballroom. This addition was built on the Commissioners' sewer, and the proposed extension would take the building further in the same direction.'

Not surprisingly, Cllr Joseph McArd spoke up for Collinson's cause but the plans were rejected and the proposed extension never built.

This might have seemed like Round One to The Hut and George Trustrum but things had not been going so well for his enterprise either.

George's grandson, Nick Keig, is well known on the Isle of Man as a world-renowned yachtsman, winning many prestigious races and also coming runner up in the Single-Handed Transatlantic Yacht Race in 1980, in a catamaran he built himself. The Isle of Man Post Office even produced a stamp issue in his honour.

Nick was born in 1936 and spent his early summers with his grandparents in Port Erin. He said he had always understood that his grandfather had 'lost a lot of money on his investment in Bradda Glen'.

Certainly, Trustrum had already put it up for sale by public auction on September 5th 1923 but Ted Collinson had bided his time on that occasion and it did not sell.

Ted might have been playing it cool or he might have been slightly overextended himself. In 1925, Collinson's Café was mortgaged for £4,500 and a newspaper report stated that: 'very large sums have been spent since the formation of the company on a Dance Room at the Port Erin branch and on reconstruction at Greensills Café'.

This may very well have been the case but the mortgage may have also been taken out for another reason. When The Hut was again offered for sale by public auction that same year, Ted Collinson made his move. On June 5th 1925 the *Isle of Man Examiner* reported that Collinson's had bought The Hut.

It went on: 'Collinson's have plans as to the future development of the resort, but at this late hour in the day, it will be impossible to carry these ideas into fruition for the present summer.'

From then on, having dealt with the upstart competition on their doorstep, Collinson's was on a roll....

Port Erin Promenade in 1923. Collinson's Café is behind the distant block of buildings on the left. *Courtesy of Peter Fisher.*

We might consider it too dangerous to walk a dog in the middle of the road outside Collinson's today, but people were made of sterner stuff in the past. *Courtesy of Peter Fisher.*

Port Erin from Bradda Head, as photographed on a
contemporary postcard: note Collinson's in the centre.

Chapter Five

GOLDEN DAYS

The layout of Port Erin in the 1920s and 1930s was, and remains, fairly simple.

There is the bay with its wide sandy beach, promenade and the harbour at one end. The road rises steeply from the lower promenade into the main part of the village where the shops are laid out along two parallel roads: Station Road, where Port Erin steam railway station is to be found, and Church Road where there is, as you might expect, the village's parish church, St Catherine's.

The larger hotels and boarding houses (mostly now converted into apartments) are situated on the upper promenade, above the bay. Holidaymakers would disembark from the ferry in Douglas and travel by steam train down to Port Erin, where they would be met at the station by a porter from the hotel they were booked into. He came in a horse-drawn cart and took their luggage up the road to the hotel and they followed on foot.

A little further along the upper promenade the road bends around the headland and you arrive at Spaldrick Bay and Bradda. This area would have been well worth making the steady climb up the road from the village to reach as it encompassed the swimming baths, Collinson's Café and the small beach below it, and now Bradda Glen with its café and beautiful walks.

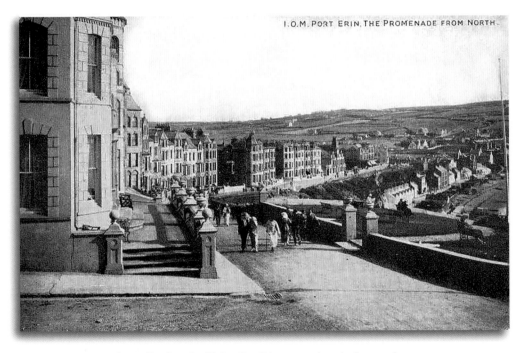

Descending from Bradda into Port Erin proper, along the Promenade.

It was described in one guidebook as being 'a setting so lovely as to make those who see it for the first time gasp with delight'.

Alice Kellett came to live in Port Erin in 1911 when her parents bought a hotel on the upper promenade. She left school at 17 and went to work there. Her memories were recalled in an interview in 1996 with Rosemary Walters for the Manx Heritage Foundation.

When asked about the type of visitor Port Erin attracted, Alice said: 'We didn't have factory workers in Port Erin. I think they were more interested in Douglas. We used to get young typists, secretaries and shop girls and families – a good mixture really – a lot of very nice families...

'There were families with young children under school age and they used to come in June because there was a reduction for children – it was out of season. And they were followed by the grown-ups, who were young people, I should say aged anything from twenty to fifty, and most of these people were active and enjoyed outdoor pursuits. They would play golf and tennis and walk and dance.

'[The] wonderful large open-air pool with diving platforms, that was very popular – a lot of seating accommodation up the grassy banks. The banks had been formed into tiers of seats and it was very cheap to sit in one of those. Oh yes and there were a lot of competitions, swimming and diving competitions: plate diving competitions were very popular... there would be plates and things flung in the pool and you had to dive down to the bottom and fish them up... And they had greasy pole competitions!'

There was very little about the entrance of the Café to suggest the extraordinary spectacle on the other side of the establishment. *Courtesy of Peter Fisher.*

Collinson's Café from the Bradda Road. *Courtesy of Peter Fisher.*

As we can see from photographs at the time, the view of Collinson's Café from the road was not – apart from the distinctive domed roof – especially striking. But imagine how it must have taken people's breath away when they visited for the first time and stepped through the door to see the ballroom open up ahead of them, the music and the dancers and the semi-circular wall of glass looking out over the sea. It would almost have been like going onboard one of the great ocean-going liners of the day.

The Port Erin Commissioners' Guide Book of 1930 described Collinson's as having 'a magnificent ballroom with a maple sprung floor [that] provides delightful facilities for dancing' and it goes on 'delightfully situated on the cliffside with its own grounds extending down to the beach, it commands one of the finest sea views in the British Isles'.

Not surprisingly it was very popular.

According to Alice Kellett: 'There was always dancing every night at Collinson's Café. There was a beautiful sprung floor there and a resident orchestra. But people used to change mostly into evening dress if they were going to Collinson's for the night to dance. You would see them trailing up the promenade in long dresses.'

Describing the sort of dancing that was popular, Alice went on: 'It was just ordinary ballroom dancing and eightsome reels – which the Scots used to enjoy – yes, barn dance, valetta, waltz, one-step, foxtrot.'

She also described the tea dances, held earlier in the day at Collinson's: 'The orchestra played and you could dance and there were tables round the ballroom and you could have afternoon tea.

'Collinson's was the Mecca and on the last night of the tourist season The Melliah was held there, a great party with balloons and streamers and Auld Lang Syne. Great fun!' A Melliah is the Manx celebration of harvest when gifts of food are brought and auctioned off for a good cause. There is lots of music and traditional country dancing.

There was also a small row of shops on the road as you approached Collinson's Café. One of these shops sold lingerie and another was a photographic shop run by Stanley Keig. Stanley was George Trustrum's son-in-law and Nick Keig's father: he would go on to build what became the largest photographic company on the island.

In the days before digital photography and camera phones, photo shops and kiosks in seaside resorts were big business.

Nick Keig remembers: 'My dad had two seasonal shops on Douglas promenade and two more in Port Erin, in Spaldrick and Station Road.

'We used to have a roving photographer who would go around Douglas and Port Erin, snapping anybody and everybody, with or without their permission. Several of my friends were among those caught out.

'These photographs proved to be a bit of a money-spinner as our two shops in Port Erin were managed by a Miss Jones, who could sell anything and who exploited the more candid shots to the full.

Forthcoming Events

SEPTEMBER 9th (Monday). — British Legion Carnival; Port Erin Branch. Annual Whist Drive and Dance. Collinson's Cafe, Port Erin. Whist 8 p.m. prompt. Dancing 8 p.m. to 12. Admission — Two Shillings.
SEPTEMBER 21st—Elementary Schools Athletic Association, Sports Festival, Cunningham's Camp Sports Field.
OCTOBER 3rd (Thursday). — Lower Foxdale Annual Yn Cruinnaght.
NOVEMBER 14th.—Douglas Allotment Ass'n—Annual Show, Villa Marina.

Four hours of entertainment for two shillings – what a bargain! This notice in the *Green Final* from September 1935 shows the kind of events on offer at Collinson's Café.

'She would never hesitate to display them very prominently in the window, often showing people who had been caught with the wrong partner. Not surprisingly, these pictures tended to sell well and very quickly.'

The wall on the road from the promenade, a few paces down from the Café. *Courtesy of Peter Fisher.*

The Café was the place to be in Port Erin: no wonder this woman is looking wistfully across to the veranda. *Courtesy of Peter Fisher.*

Clearly with a large chain of shops in the north of England and his new chocolate venture, Ted Collinson did not have the time to concern himself with the day to day running of the Isle of Man cafés.

He had earlier appointed Vincent Theodore Ainley to open his Douglas cafés and both they and the Port Erin venues appear to have thrived under his management.

In March 1926, 'Vint', as he was known, was applying to the Castletown Licensing Court for a 'sweets' licence, that is a licence to serve British wines and champagne, for both Collinson's Café in Port Erin and the Bradda Glen café. At the court, Vint stated that there was 'a substantial demand for these British wines, especially champagne, principally with meals.'

Vint was given a bit of a grilling at this point by Mr J. D. Qualtrough who wanted to know his full history. To this Vint replied that he 'had had 25 years' experience of the business. Up to three years ago he managed the Wellington Hall Café, and since then he had been general manager of all the firm's [Collinson's] places.

He went on to say that: 'They only engaged experienced waitresses; they did not employ young girls. These places were only open from Whit-Week to the end of September. The wines to be sold were champagne, sherry, cider, port, and Whiteway's ginger wine.'

He added that many of their customers assumed they already had a licence and asked for 'light wines' but 'the greatest demand is for champagne'.

'That is not a British wine,' snorted Mr Qualtrough.

To which Vint replied: 'There is a British champagne.'

Vint Ainley appears to have had a good standard of living. He and his wife had a substantial house on Peel Road in Douglas. We do not know her name but apparently Vint's success had been achieved 'with the great help of his wife, who was also his helpmate in business'.

She also apparently kept up her social connections in their native Yorkshire: she was featured in a publication there, the *Forget Me Not* magazine, which was describing various styles of hats sold by an upmarket milliner's. It mentions 'a good-sized, turban-shaped, seal hat with the upturned brim finished with an Oriental beaded ornament on the left side which was desired by Mrs G Ainley of Collinson's Café, Port Erin, Isle of Man'.

Keith McArd remembered a Mr Paul Buckingham making frequent visits to the island from the Collinson's HQ, to check on the progress of building works and maintenance at the Port Erin café. Keith recalled him chiefly because he drove a distinctive Morgan three wheeler car.

But Paul Buckingham was more than just a Collinson's employee, he was family, as his daughter, Kate Firth, explained: 'My father, Paul Buckingham, was a nephew by marriage of Edward Collinson. In the 1930s he also joined the family business and I can recall him talking often about Ted.

'My father lived with Ted and his wife for many years and he learned all about the catering and the tea and coffee tasting and blending. Ted swanned around in a Rolls Royce and seemed to have been very generous: they definitely weren't without.

'My dad spent a lot of time in Port Erin as he was the manager of Bradda Glen before and after the war.'

Paul Buckingham, manager of Bradda Glen around the time of the First World War. *Courtesy of Kate Firth.*

By this time Collinson's was already moving into offering holiday accommodation. In March 1929 the *Examiner* informed its readers that 'it is proposed by the proprietors to establish a camp for young men in "The Hut" grounds during the summer, and this gives rise to the necessity for proper sanitary arrangements.'

Naturally this led to more long discussions by Port Erin Commissioners who continued to be a thorn in Collinson's side, and probably vice versa.

It is often the case in a small community that a successful company like Collinson's, though it was providing facilities for tourists to enjoy and employing local people, was still regarded as the 'outsider'. Whatever they did would be subject to more scrutiny as they would, according to this line of thinking, inevitably try to take advantage of the locals at some point.

The fact that the Manx themselves are quite a canny bunch, especially in property matters, does not seem to have weighed in the equation.

This feeling seems to have applied especially to Collinson's Port Erin café as it was a venue that the locals themselves didn't get a chance to use very often: it was closed during the winter and, in the summer, most of them were far too busy looking after the holidaymakers to have time to go out drinking tea and dancing.

The Collinson's Cafés in Douglas, on the other hand, were open all year round and appear to have been very popular with people living on the island. The Duke Street café in particular had a function room where many formal dinners, weddings and meetings of local organisations and societies were held.

Collinson's Cafe cutlery.
Courtesy of Kate Firth

64

In Port Erin it was a different story and the animosity there was clearly demonstrated in 1930 when an application from Collinson's for music and dancing licences in respect of the café and Bradda Glen was being considered.

"THE THATCHED HOUSE." BRADDA GLEN.   One of the approaches

COLLINSON'S
BRADDA GLEN HOLIDAY CENTRE.
PORT ERIN, I.O.M.

Bradda Glen is not a Camp. It is a Holiday Estate, owned and served by the proprietors of Collinson's Cafés, which are not only the best known and most efficient in the Isle of Man, but are also famous throughout the North of England.

Framed in the most beautiful setting in the Island, the estate occupies the whole of the North side of Port Erin Bay and looks right across the Irish Sea; where the mountains of Mourne, 50 miles away, can often be seen.

Semi-tropical plants and palms flourish—red and purple-flowering fuchsias form the hedges—a lovely lawn backed by trees and facing South surrounds the Thatched House, Lounge, and Dining Room. Here you can sit at your ease or sunbathe to your heart's content, soothed by music and lulled by the waves.

Beyond the four hard tennis courts, (FREE to those staying on the estate), a delightful cliff path, between hedges of fuchsia, and close to the sea, opens on to the "wild"—where heather, gorse, thyme, thrift and bracken flourish at their own sweet will; and where rugged cliffs sweep down to the most limpid, clear sea you can imagine. This "wild," with all its natural charm, extends over half a mile to a great cleft on Bradda Head, where the path swings back at a higher level, with an extensive view of the cliffs and Port Erin Bay.

This is all yours, on your very own doorstep—a setting so lovely as to make those who see it for the first time gasp with delight. Nowhere in Britain is such a situation available for Holidays except at an extravagant price;—nowhere in the Isle of Man can one be had to compare with Bradda Glen at any price whatever.

A brochure for Bradda Glen Holiday Centre is adamant that it "is not a camp". *Courtesy of Peter Fisher.*

The licence for the café was granted unanimously but, regarding the Glen, a petition had been presented by local ratepayers for the licence to be refused because of the noise. They complained that 'during the last fortnight the noise had been going on incessantly and become a bigger nuisance than ever'.

The ensuing discussion led to an outburst from the chairman, Mr J. S. Kermode, who declared: 'When anything has come up around this table in the last twelve months affecting Collinson's, whether buildings, plans or drainage, some members have let their own pettifogging grievances come into it.'

Nonetheless, Collinson's pressed on with their development and, once again, appear to have provided a very special venue which looked to appeal to the upper end of the market. Its own brochures stated: 'Bradda Glen is not a camp. It is a Holiday centre of the best kind, owned and served by Collinson's, the well known caterers, who know good taste and whose primary object here is to ensure the comfort and wellbeing of every guest... Bradda Glen offers you a holiday a millionaire might envy at a price you can afford'.

Facilities included a recreation room with ping pong tables and space for music and dancing and four hard tennis courts. It later expanded, at a reported cost of around £3,000, to include bungalows for married couples and family parties and a ladies' hostel. This allowed the venue to accommodate up to 250 people. It appears to have been very popular and regularly played host to, amongst others, parties of young Americans on cultural tours of Europe.

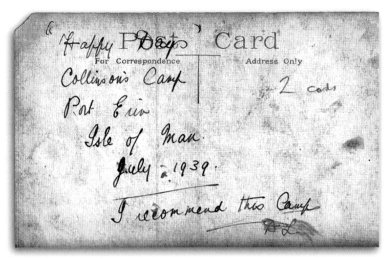

The Holiday Centre was popular, but they were less successful in persuading people not to call it a camp, as this 1939 postcard demonstrates. *Courtesy of Peter Fisher.*

This undated poster for "Bradda Holiday Camp" reveals Collinson's eventual admission of defeat in the branding battle. *Courtesy of Peter Fisher.*

Georg Meier with his historic BMW twin-cylinder Grand Prix race machine on which won the 1939 Senior Isle of Man TT race.

Chapter Six

A Different Kind of Visitor

For the first half of 1939 life continued pretty much as normal on the Isle of Man. The holidaymakers still arrived, and Collinson's Café and Bradda Glen continued to be popular venues. In June the island's famous TT motorcycle races went ahead with many competitors from Europe taking part.

Ironically the most important race of the meeting, the Senior TT, was won by a German rider, Georg Meier, on a supercharged 500CC BMW Type 255 motorcycle.

It was the last time the races would be held until 1947. In September 1939 World War II started and its effects began to be felt.

On Friday September 8th 1939 the *Ramsey Courier* carried the following notice:

'The public are notified that on and after Thursday 7th September, persons travelling from the Isle of Man to ports in Great Britain, Eire or Northern Ireland must be in possession of a travel permit (or valid passport which must be endorsed at the Travel Permit Division, Government Office, Douglas).'

This was met by an immediate outcry from the Manx public who had never previously had to produce a passport or any other sort of document when travelling to the UK mainland.

The *Isle of Man Times* denounced it as a 'scandal'.

On October 4th, the UK Government backed down and the Home Secretary announced in the House of Commons that the system of travel permits to and from the Isle of Man would not be continued.

But the public, and the tourism industry, had bigger travel issues to worry about than the minor inconvenience of having to obtain a permit. Speaking at a shareholders' meeting a few months later, the chairman of Isle of Man Steam Packet, described the end of the 1939 summer season, saying: 'Everything augured well, our fleet was in full commission and in splendid running order... then the war began, and in a day or two traffic ended. Our largest and best steamers were, of course, required for national purposes, and are still so required.'

Although the company managed to maintain regular winter services with the vessels left to them, the fares went up, along with the cost of transporting cargo to the island. Air services to and from the island were also affected by the war, due to the shortage of pilots.

Then, in May 1940 two events occurred which would really bring home to everyone on the island the extent to which war was changing their lives.

The first was Dunkirk.

As we know from our history lessons, May 26th – June 4th saw the evacuation of 338,000 Allied troops from Dunkirk.

Less widely known is that, of these, 24,000 were picked up and returned to England by Isle of Man Steam Packet passenger ships. These were manned by ferry staff more used to carrying crowds of exuberant holidaymakers; all of them had volunteered for this very different and dangerous service.

A number of them were decorated for their bravery including the captain of the *Lady of Mann* which took part in the evacuations at Dunkirk, Le Havre, Cherbourg, and La Pallice.

On May 29th, three of the company's ships were lost: at 5.30am, *Mona's Queen* III, making her second journey into Dunkirk, hit a mine, broke in two and sank with the loss of 24 crew. Later that day *Fenella* II and *King Orry* IV were bombed. In total 45 men lost their lives. Most of them were from Douglas but two were from Port St Mary and one was from Port Erin.

The *Ramsey Courier* commented: 'Nothing that has happened during the course of the war has brought the terrible conflict nearer to our island.'

On the very same day, just as news of this tragedy was sinking in, 3,000 mostly German and Austrian internees disembarked from the ferry and travelled south to Port Erin and Port St Mary by steam train and bus, where they were to be accommodated for the foreseeable future by local hoteliers and boarding house keepers.

Women aliens embarking at Liverpool for internment on the Isle of Man.

The timing could hardly have been worse, and it wasn't helped by the situation in the village being understandably slightly chaotic at first.

Bertha Bracey, who visited the camp, wrote in the *Manchester Guardian*, 'Look for a moment at the position as it faced the commandant of the women's camp in May 1940. Within 48 hours of arriving at the Rushen peninsula she, with five helpers, had to receive three thousand women and children.

'Not even the names of the internees were known to her, still less any information about ages, family units, state of health, or status.

'Hotels, boarding-houses, and private houses had arranged to receive different numbers of internees. With the help of some of the local clergy, women and children were counted out, ordered in groups, and sent off to billets.

'The double bed seems to be a system throughout the Isle of Man, so it was no fault of the commandant if sick and healthy, Nazi and anti-Nazi women and children were found sharing rooms and even beds.'

At first the locals thought that, because they spoke German, their new guests were all Nazis. They soon discovered that the majority were Jewish refugees who had fled the Nazi regime and realised that they had no quarrel with them.

So, whatever their initial feelings might have been following Dunkirk, they took note that the camp commandant had asked them to treat the new arrivals with kindness and they appear to have done so.

No doubt the hoteliers and boarding house landladies were also pleased at the prospect of being paid by the Home Office to feed and house their new guests all year round, where before they had only enjoyed revenue during the short summer season.

Barbara Eaton had fled Germany with her Jewish father in January 1939 and was among the first batch of internees to arrive. She was

16 at the time and she later recalled her experiences when she was interviewed in 1979 for the Imperial War Museum: 'When we first came here we were fortunate in having really splendid June weather, real holiday weather. Though it was a very serious matter to be interned, when you are very young you don't take it all so tragically and to me there was a holiday flavour about the whole thing.'

That holiday mood among the internees lingered for the next few months: during the summer of 1940, the weather was glorious and the beach was crowded every day with internee women and their children, playing in the sand and bathing in the sea.

But they were still, at the end of it all, being detained and their lives were necessarily restricted, as were the lives of the people of Port Erin.

The most obvious symbol of this was the erection of a tall barbed wire fence around the village with two control points going in and out. Collinson's Café and Bradda Glen were both inside the wire.

Further up the road from Collinson's, the residents on the hillside above Bradda Glen were outside the wire and had restricted access to the village.

A group of interned women in lessons. *Courtesy of Manx National Heritage.*

'The people of Port Erin are up in arms about the unnecessary restrictions imposed on people living in the district outside the camp area, who are unable to shop in the village and unable to attend the cinema in the evenings,' thundered the *Isle of Man Times* in January 1941.

There were all sorts of other rules and regulations that had to be followed and the locals fell foul of them too. Soldiers and sailors returning to Port Erin or Port St Mary on leave were sometimes delayed for hours at the barrier to the camp because they omitted to obtain the necessary police permit in Douglas.

The detainees at Port Erin had considerable freedom. These three women seem to have decided on a leisurely walk through town. *Published in "Friend or Foe" by Rushen Heritage Trust.*

A local estate agent and insurance broker was brought up before the High Bailiff for taking a parcel from a young internee into Douglas to be posted and a fisherman in Port St Mary was prosecuted for giving another internee a packet of six cigarettes.

Bradda Glen was used to house internees, including a number of nuns, whilst Collinson's Café had several different functions during the war years.

There is only so long that people can spend idling their time away on the beach. Many of the internees were keen to work and had impressive skills and talents to share.

For the older children like Barbara Eaton, and the adults, education classes were held in the ballroom at Collinson House.

Barbara Eaton recalled: 'I put my name down for morning classes in English, Maths, Latin and shorthand.

'There were some splendid people there with teaching experience, people from the arts and people with lecturing experience. I got the opportunity to mix with people who were far superior in intellect and knowledge and I really think it laid the foundations to a lot of things.

'I think it's one of the great positives of that period [that] I had the opportunity to mix with some outstanding people, some very special people.'

There are also reports of puppet shows and songs for children at Collinson's Café and events for adults.

'At the educational centre at Collinson's Café, Port Erin, last Friday, Miss Mona Douglas gave the postponed lecture-recital on Manx folk songs and dances before an audience of upwards of 100 women and children internees.'

WOMAN ALIEN DENIES ALLEGATIONS

All Well Treated

RUSHEN

"Punch Frees a Fairy" was the title of a puppet show and songs for children given at the internment camp at Collinson's Cafe, Port Erin, on Thursday afternoon.

Mr. F. C. Lowcock, Ballakneale, Port Erin, has received a letter from the general secretary of the British Sailors' Society, thanking him for a cheque for £15-4-0 — the proceeds of a recent whist drive, and stating how much they appreciate the kindness of Mrs. Lowcock and her helpers for organising the event.

RUSHEN

The Rev. Harry Johnson gave an impressive address at the meeting of Port St. Mary Christian Endeavour held in Mount Tabor Methodist Schoolroom on Wednesday night. The leader was Miss J. Carine, and the soloist, Miss Bessie Kneen.

At the educational centre at Collinson's Cafe, Port Erin, last Friday, Miss Mona Douglas gave the postponed lecture-recital on Manx folk songs and dances before an audience of upwards of 100 women and children internees. The lecture was most informative. The observations of a lady internee, who is devoting her time in work amongst the children, was that the lecture was very interesting, and captivated the appreciation of all.

Courtesy of Isle of Man Examiner

When Christmas 1940 came, internees were invited to Collinson's Café each day during the festive season and coffee, cakes, biscuits, fruit and salad were served 'at the usual moderate prices'.

The internee women were also allowed to meet with husbands who were interned at the male camps around the island. Their first meeting, in July 1940, had taken place at the Ballaqueeney Hotel in Port St Mary, but subsequent meetings took place at Collinson's Café.

The men were brought under military escort and, according to posters at the time, were allowed just half an hour with their spouses. Coffee was provided but wines and spirits were not.

Later, in May 1941, a married camp was established in Port St Mary and some of the women from Port Erin were moved there to live with their husbands.

When it came to working, a system, known as the Service Exchange, was set up among the internees with the blessing of the camp commandant, through which services such as laundry and hairdressing were provided in exchange for token money.

This cardigan was knitted by Else Forner for her daughter Ingrid, using recycled wool (and recycled wood for the buttons). Both were interned on the Isle of Man during the Second World War.
© *Manx National Heritage (2008-0336).*

This came about because, whilst some of the internees were comparatively wealthy, others arrived on the island virtually penniless. Even the wealthier ones were limited as to how much money they could withdraw from their accounts.

According to the *Examiner*: 'There is an embargo on an internee drawing more than 5s a week from her account without the permission of the Camp Commandant, and purchases of sweets, cigarettes, small toilet articles, newspapers and other such items must be met from this sum.

'Internees are forbidden to obtain credit from shops or to purchase alcoholic drink, or to buy or use electric torches, candles, spirit lamps or methylated spirits. Their purchase of electric light bulbs is also forbidden.'

Ira Rischowski, another internee interviewed in 1979 for the Imperial War Museum archive recalled: 'The wealthier women did not want to do their own washing but there were plenty of domestic servants that were only too pleased to earn a little bit of money... a system of token money was evolved.'

She went on: 'The question then arose as to what you could do with your token money. Some internees were very good bakers and the existing café, the Collinson's Café, which was on the promenade, I don't know how it came about but eventually the Collinson's Café was taken over by the [camp] supervisors and put at the disposal of the internees and this is where you could buy a cup of coffee.

'I don't know whether it was real coffee, in those days I doubt it very much.

'And you could also eat very, very good cake, baked by the internees, paid for with the token money.

'I occasionally frequented the Collinson's Café but the first summer [1940] was so glorious that I spent most of the time in the open air.'

Predictably, as the war dragged on and especially during the Blitz, a fair degree of resentment arose in England at what was perceived as the favourable conditions the internees were enjoying. The tabloid press was only too happy to stoke this resentment by suggesting that the Isle of Man hotels should be cleared of internees and given instead as accommodation to those who had been bombed out of their homes.

George Slocombe, writing in the [UK] *Sunday Express*, a national paper, in March 1941, describes paying a visit to Port Erin: 'I did, indeed,

Interned children exercising on Port Erin beach during the Second World War. *Courtesy of Manx National Heritage.*

succeed in penetrating the camp under escort, in company with two colleagues and in a blizzard of snow and sleet as disconcerting as the camp commandant's attitude.

'We walked for a quarter of a mile through one of the streets of her closely defended town. We passed many women aliens, warmly clad, some of them in furs, most of them wearing slacks. They seemed in good health and well-nourished, and not at all in low spirits.

'They live in one of the most beautiful parts of the Island, with sea bathing possible until late in the year, and they are billeted in rooms for which in peace time a guinea a day was charged.'

The truth is that both sides of the arrangement, internees and locals, appear to have made the best of the situation. Many of the landladies formed friendships with the internees staying with them and continued to correspond after their release.

For their part the internees who spoke about their time in Port Erin have few complaints about their treatment apart from the basic fact that they were not free. A few lines from a little poem written by one internee for her landlady sums up the general feeling:

'About everything here, I was very pleased Though I hope badly to be released.'

> **HOW BRITAIN TREATS THE ALIEN.**
>
> ---
>
> **A VISIT TO THE ISLE OF MAN CAMPS.**
>
> DOUGLAS, MONDAY.
>
> We stood on the hillside beyond Greeba, in Man, surveying the whole stretch of Knockaloe Camp, the great and strange cosmopolitan town where the streets are formed of double-ribbed barbed-wire, and where the compounds, for all their spaciousness, look like enormous cages without tops. Further up the hill a group of alien prisoners, attracted by the offer of reward and perhaps impelled by the monotony of camp life, were quarrying for stone; to our left another party were reclaiming a barren hill-top for a market garden; and inside the huts we had already seen hundreds of deft craftsmen plying their trades. In front of us recreation in a dozen different forms was in full swing, and in the Twenty-two Acres, one of the three general recreation-grounds which serve the camp as a whole, and which only supplement a fairly liberal provision in each of the compounds.

Report in Manchester Guardian.

The door opening up to the veranda at Collinson's.
© *Manx National Heritage (PG/13633/1/1978/129/1)*

Chapter Seven

END OF A DYNASTY

Tourism during the war had virtually ground to a halt, aside from the few stout souls prepared to brave a ferry journey that included looking out for mines in Liverpool Bay and the sight of barbed wire in front of many of the hotels housing internees on Douglas promenade.

Port Erin, as we have seen, had been completely off limits, but after the last of the internees departed in 1945 it was time for the village to go back to being a tourist destination once more.

For Collinson's that meant some changes to their business.

In February 1945 a front-page report in the *Examiner*, entitled 'Commissioner's Ambitious Step', signalled the local authorities' intention to buy Bradda Glen holiday camp from Collinson's.

Subsequent reports revealed Port Erin Commissioners' concern about 'spoliation by undesirable development' and their wish to 'remove certain existing hut buildings at an early date, as these impaired the natural beauty' of the site.

The 'spoliation' of the island had been a topic for discussion for a number of years. In 1942 the chairman of the Manx Development Board, Mr W. B. Corrin had made an address on the subject which stated as one of its aims the purchase of all the glens around the island.

He said: 'It has often been a source of annoyance to many of our visitors that our glens and beauty spots have been forbidden to them. That private enterprise has demanded a toll from all those who would explore some of our most beautiful glens. It is time we had sense enough to bring this state of things to an end.

'I am glad to inform you that steps have been taken to inquire into the possibility of acquiring our glens and opening them free to our visitors.'

This of course included Bradda Glen for which an entry charge was then being made.

The Commissioners needed to ask Tynwald for approval for the purchase and for leave to borrow the £20,000 required to buy it. It also meant an additional sixpenny rate for the people of Port Erin.

For Collinson's it would have been a good deal: after several years of housing internees and little money spent on maintenance, a significant investment would undoubtedly be needed in the site.

And besides, Ted Collinson, now in his sixties, had other plans in mind.

Ted Collinson as an older man. *Courtesy of Kate Firth.*

Ted Collinson with his daughter Elizabeth. *Courtesy of Kate Firth.*

By 1946, despite coal shortages and rationing, it looked as though the island was rapidly returning to the sort of tourist boom it had enjoyed before the war. The ferry services were carrying near-record numbers of passengers and the TT races in June were attracting increasing numbers of spectators and competitors.

At the 25th annual meeting of Collinsons (I.O.M.) Ltd it was stated that the company had had 'easily the best years in the company's history' during the war, 'largely due to the busy time experienced by the firm as caterers for Services personnel'.

As the lease was nearly up on the Duke Street café they had acquired property on the opposite side of the street, encompassing several shops and the former Empire Theatre and they planned to build 'a super structure that would be a credit to the company and an asset to the Isle of Man'.

The company was in a strong financial position and looked to be going from strength to strength.

So, for the last half of that decade it appeared that the war had been a mere interruption to the tourism boom and things would carry on much as they had before. Visitors were still arriving in huge numbers: 1946 saw the second-highest ever, just behind the record in 1913.

But visitors were starting to fall out of love with the Isle of Man and the signs were there. An increasing number of complaints were received about the standard of food and the value for money in the island's boarding houses. They did have the excuse that it was not easy offering a gourmet visitor experience whilst rationing was still in force, but it was also highly likely that the many years of success had made them complacent. They had begun to take their visitors for granted and hadn't noticed that other destinations might have more to offer.

In July 1946, *Mona's Herald* reported on two very similar court cases, both on the same day, involving parking offences. A trivial matter but the individuals involved were prominent local businessmen and both of them used their appearances in court to criticise Douglas' 'chaotic' parking.

One of them was Vint Ainley, the Collinson's manager, who was charged with parking his car outside the Greensill's Corner Café. He said he had been called to the café to help regulate a long queue of customers outside the café, waiting to get in. When told he was being reported he had replied: 'It is a pity you haven't something better to do.'

The High Bailiff was having none of it and imposed a fine of 10s.

The other man prosecuted was a Mr Thomas Harold Colebourn who, a decade later, would play a significant role in the story of Collinson House.

T. H. Colebourn, a radio engineer, had served in the Signals in the First World War and had been shot and blinded in one eye. He opened a shop selling electrical and white goods in Victoria Street Douglas in 1924, shortly after the start of public service broadcasting, and manufactured 'wireless sets' under the brand name of Cleartone.

He had also used his radio engineering expertise to good effect in the Second World War when German bombers were flying up the Irish Sea targeting key cities like Liverpool.

T. H. COLEBOURN.
Stand 14.

Mr T. H. Colebourn's interest in wireless dates from 1917, when serving in the B.E.F. in France. He was in the "Secret Signal Section of the Wireless Corps," and was unable to continue with the Marconi Company after the war, on account of loss of right eye, owing to gunshot wound.

Commenced selling wireless sets twelve years ago, in partnership with Mr N. C. Kermode. The partnership was dissolved by mutual consent two years ago.

He has lately taken over large show—

Mr. T. H. COLEBOURN.

T. H. Colebourn in a newspaper profile from the mid-1930s.

A consignment of Murphy Radios being delivered at Mr. T. H. Colebourn's Establishment.

Modern living was not complete without a high-tech radio: Mr Colebourn's shop was the contemporary equivalent of the Apple Store. *Isle of Man Times*, 1938.

His grandson, Phil Colebourn, who now runs the business, explained: 'He realised the Germans were using Radio Athlone [the Irish national broadcaster and predecessor to RTÉ] to work their distances out so he re-broadcast Radio Athlone from the Isle of Man at different times and they were working out their distances from there and dropping their bombs in the sea.

'He got away with that for about three weeks and saved an awful lot of lives.'

And so the decade rolled on and Collinson's Café in Port Erin continued to play host to tea dances, whist drives and other entertainments.It was also popular with local ladies who enjoyed a round of golf at the nearby Rowany course before going into Collinson's for afternoon tea.

Evening dances were still held there too. Nina Shimmin, who grew up at the nearby Waverley Hotel says: 'I have memories of being put to bed as a toddler, but then standing on the windowsill watching people coming to Collinson's dressed up for dancing, as one did then.

'My bedroom window was in the peak of the gable and I was small enough to be able to stand on the windowsill and look out and see the people coming up from the promenade, all dressed up.'

But Collinson's (IOM) was about to be hit by two major blows, which occurred within a year of each other.

In November 1948, Vint Ainley, Collinson's very able Isle of Man manager, died at the age of 65. Among the many tributes one described him as 'one of the best-known businessmen in Douglas'.

It went on: 'A Yorkshireman, and proud of it, "Vint" Ainley started Collinson's business in Douglas over 30 years ago. and his energy, zeal and business acumen built up the very flourishing catering business which exists to-day'.

Death of Mr V. T. Ainley

One of the best-known business men in Douglas, Mr Vincent T. Ainley, manager and director of Collinson's (I.O.M.) Ltd., died on Friday at home, "Brow," Peel Road, Douglas. A Yorkshireman, and proud of it, "Vint" Ainley started Col- linson's busi- ness in Dou- glas over 30 years ago, and his energy, zeal and business acumen built up the very flourishing catering business which exists to-day, with the great help of his wife, who was also his helpmate in business.

Mr Ainley, who was 65, had one great interest outside his business ,and that was the Manx Grand Prix. He was one of those who were in at the birth of the old Amateur T.T., and he had been a member of the M.M.C.C. Committee, organisers of that race and its successor, the Manx Grand Prix, since the September

The obituary of V. T. Ainley.

The following year came more bad news with the disappearance of their chairman Ted Collinson, now 70. A keen amateur geologist, he had been out fossil hunting near Scarborough. A search party with a pair of bloodhounds was sent out to look for him.

A few days later coastguards spotted his body at the foot of a 200ft cliff.

An inquest concluded that he had been wearing smooth-soled shoes and had apparently slipped. His injuries were consistent with a fall and a book on the geology of Yorkshire had been found near the body.

In February 1950, the *Isle of Man Examiner* published Ted's will. He left £5,000 and an annuity to his daughter, Miss Elizabeth Collinson, asking her to 'remember that these businesses are the result of the sustained effort of three generations. Between them they have built up the Collinson tradition with its happy family atmosphere, its sense of human values, justice, and fair play.'

In June that year, for the first time, Collinson's reported a reduced dividend and in September storms of such severity shook the island that windows in Collinson's Cafe, Port Erin, were blown in.

It was an omen.

Visitor numbers were slumping, as they had in many other British resorts. The five-day week had come into operation and that, coupled with the fact that petrol now was off ration, led to speculation that people might be taking advantage of these factors for more weekend activities just a car journey away.

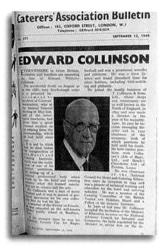

The obituary of Ted Collinson.

It was also thought that the uncertainty of world affairs, including the war in Korea, might be deterring people from taking holidays.

The *Ramsey Courier* commented: 'It is a position that is extremely difficult to weigh up, but one lesson is to be learned from it all, and that is that all parties in the Isle of Man must pull together and do their utmost to attract and satisfy visitors.

'The catering for holiday-makers is no side-line in the Isle of Man. Apart from agriculture and fishing and smaller avenues of employment there is no other industry. The island's economy is based on a full visiting season: if that fails, everybody is affected.'

The golden days of tourism were definitely over.

See Yourself on Television

In 1956, T H Colebourn brought television cameras to the Isle of Man for the first time, and allowed members of the public to see themselves live on screen. Here, he is featured in the *Isle of Man Examiner* to promote the event.

Chapter Eight

NEW OWNERS

The 1950s might have brought gloom on the tourism front but it also brought television and, in 1953, a new Queen was about to be crowned.

Ever the innovator, T H Colebourn had been trying for a number of years to get the Isle of Man Government to build a transmitter, only to be told that television was 'a flash in the pan'. In the end he took matters into his own hands as his grandson, Phil, explains: 'He did a deal with the farmer who owned The Howe on the Old Castletown Road and he built his own transmitter, without permission, in order to broadcast the Coronation of the Queen.

'He then invited all the MHKs [members of the House of Keys, analogous to British MPs] in government to the shop in Douglas where he set up the first television set. They all came, they all had a lot to drink and watched the coverage, and he was never asked to take the transmitter down.'

Colebourn then purchased the plot of land for thirty guineas and built a much larger transmitter to which the BBC, ITV and Channel Four all added their hardware. Fifty years later it proved a nice legacy for Phil when the government made it the subject of a compulsory purchase order and, after much wrangling as to whether it was still 'agricultural' land, Phil was paid what he describes as 'a handsome fee' for it.

Following the death of Vint Ainley, Edith Fullerton took over as manageress of the Collinson venues on the island.

Spaldrick Bay, Port Erin. *Reproduced by kind permission of The Falcon's Nest Hotel, Port Erin.*

Her son Bryan, who is now 82, remembers it as a very special time.

'I was about 12 and I spent every summer up at Collinson's. It was closed in the winter and my mum would be working in Douglas but in the summer she would be in Port Erin. She would sleep in the bedroom on the right and my Auntie Marjorie who was a waitress had the bedroom on the left.

'They had a serving place downstairs and another one upstairs to serve people inside and on the balcony.

'I slept in the ballroom on a bench: it was lovely waking up and looking out of those big windows. It was just like you were living at home: it was so cosy even though it was so big. I can remember just about everything about the place. I keep telling my grandchildren what a lovely building it was.

'I used to spend many hours on the balcony watching the fishing boats go out or I would go to the golf course across the road and pay 1s and you'd get a ball and a club to use for that. There was also a bike place on the block of shops by the café that hired bikes and another of my aunties had a shop there that sold china.

'I also spent my time down at the baths. When they did the bathing beauty contests I'd go and sit on the bank to watch the proceedings: they came from all over to take part.

'There were two rowing boats for hire at the private beach belonging to the café, two lads looked after them, and we were allowed to take them out. When the season was over we would take them out of the water and carry them up the hill through the trees to be stored in the garage by the café.

'There was a big sign on the dome droof at the front saying Collinson's Café and two windows either side of the door. Once my mum asked me to make some 'ice creams' to put in the two windows for display so I made them with plaster of Paris and various colourings and I made wafers and a cherry to go on top.'

Splashing in the water on Port Erin beach, from a contemporary postcard. *Courtesy of Peter Fisher.*

Jennifer Quayle remembers being in dance competitions at Collinson's Cafe when she was a child. 'I was born in 1946 and I would have been seven or eight so it would have been the early 1950s.

'I came from a dancing family and I started dancing when I was two. My brother Graham and my sister Patricia both danced too. She went on to become a ballet dancer.

'I used to do old time and ballroom dancing: at that age my partner would have been another girl. We always had all our dresses made to match our partner's.

'It would have been a Saturday afternoon we went to Collinson's and it must have been the summertime because the roof opened up so half the floor would be open to the sky. It was on a sprung dancefloor too, one of the few we had on the island.

A horticultural display at Collinson's in 1955, *Isle of Man Examiner.*

'I remember it being a very beautiful place, being able to look out and see the sea.'

In keeping with the general mood of tourism gloom on the island, Collinson's (IOM) continued to report reduced profits for the next few years. In 1955 they announced that the scheme to build a new café in Duke Street had been abandoned and the site was being disposed of and in 1956, at an Extraordinary General Meeting, a resolution was passed to voluntarily wind up the company with all creditors paid in full. A local firm of accountants was appointed as liquidators.

On March 1st 1957 the *Isle of Man Times* reported that the company's largest café in Duke Street had been sold: 'Collinson's Cafe, scene of many important functions held by organisations on the island, is in the process of voluntary liquidation, and many people will have noticed with regret, and many nostalgic memories of past social functions, that the considerable property owned by the company has been on the market.

An article advertising the auction of Collinson's. From the *Isle of Man Examiner*, November 1957.

'The large premises used as a store in Myrtle Street has been sold to the Athol Garage by the liquidator, Mr H. E. Kneale, and what is known to local people as "Little Collinson's", in Duke Street, has been purchased by Mr Tomlinson, the Belvedere, Douglas. Messrs Irving Brothers of Duke Street, are taking possession of the main Duke Street cafe, and will continue the catering business which has gone on there for the many years that Collinson's were in existence.

THE FORMER COLLINSON'S CAFE at Spaldrick, Port Erin, which has been sold to a syndicate of local business men for £2,500. Mr. T. H. Colebourn, who with Mr. H. Orrell and Mr. E. Turner were the purchasers indicated that it was proposed to develop the building on lines of considerable interest in the Island.

The *Examiner* announces the Douglas businessmen's successful bid.

'For disposal are the remaining premises of the company in Fort Street and Regent Street, Douglas, and at Port Erin.'

It seems that there were few takers for Collinson's Port Erin: in November 1957 it was put up for auction with no reserve price.

The sale attracted a large audience and when the auctioneer opened the bidding at £1,000 there were several bidders. In the end, when the hammer went down, Collinson's Café Port Erin had been purchased by a syndicate of Douglas businessmen for just £2,500. The syndicate was made up of Adrian Orrell, Mr E. Turner and our old friend, T. H. Colebourn.

The latter told the *Isle of Man Times* that 'the syndicate had definite plans for the development of the property, but he could not yet disclose the nature of them.'

Mr T. H. Colebourn is clearly enjoying himself as judge of a beauty pageant at Bradda Glen. Otherwise, the syndicate made little use of their new property. From the *Isle of Man Examiner*, June 1959.

Collinson's Cafe Assessment Application

THE Assessment Board will, on Thursday week (February 20th) hear an application made for a reduction in the assessment of the former Collinsons Cafe at Spaldrick, Port Erin which is now owned by a syndicate of local businessmen.

The owners are Messrs A. Orrell, E. Turner and T. H. Colebourn and they ask for a reduction of the rateable value from £280 to £140 and the gross from £350 to £175.

The grounds of the application are the the present assessments are excessive and incorrect, and that the cafe and ballroom were not used as such during 1957 and at present are unoccupied, and that the assessments are unfair in comparison with those of similar premises.

The syndicate soon applied for a reduction in rates for Collinson's. From the *Isle of Man Examiner*, February 1958.

The May Queen is crowned at Bradda Glen, April 1962. © *Manx National Heritage (PG/13633/1/1962/151/1)*

However, at a time when television sales and rentals were booming it clearly didn't figure high on T.H.'s list of priorities – his grandson Phil was not even aware that he had ever owned it – and nothing was done to the property.

In September 1960, the Southern Snippets section of the *Isle of Man Times* reported a hot piece of local gossip: 'I hear that great plans are afoot for Collinson's, the cafe that has stood sentinel overlooking the bay in Port Erin for many a year.

'For the past three its peeling paintwork and empty eyes have been a constant reproach to all who passed by – a pathetic reminder of past glory. Now all this is to be changed. Work on the building starts in October. It is to be brought right up to date – modern decor and fitments – the lot.

'When it opens next year I hear there will be cabaret shows, "rock" sessions for the teenagers – in fact, something to suit all ages.'

But with visitor numbers to the island in ever-worsening decline, nothing ever came of it and Collinson's Café Port Erin was once again on the market.

It was finally sold in 1963 for £2,000 to Eric Vincent Cunliffe and Susan Rubino Cunliffe.

Collinson House in the Lythgoe era.
Courtesy of David Lythgoe

Chapter Nine

THE LYTHGOES

Little is known about the Cunliffes beyond what is on the conveyance document: he was a retired Squadron Leader with a flowery signature, she was a housewife. Their address is given as Plantation House, Port St Mary, but we don't know if they intended to move into Collinson's and use it as their residence or whether they also had plans to revive its glory days as a café and tea dance venue.

What we do know is that, when they sold it in 1968, their Port St Mary property, not Collinson's, was given as their former address and they had moved to Devon.

We know that the new purchasers, William and Mollie Nuttall were from Lytham St Annes and paid £7,250 for it and we also know that they moved to the island and lived there. They even changed the name to 'Water's Edge'.

Beyond that we know little, though it is unlikely they did any substantial work on the property to turn it into a home because Keith McArd, who had by then taken over the company, along with his father, does not recall doing anything to it at the time.

However, when they sold it, in 1974, it was to a family who remember the property well and with great affection.

Joseph Lythgoe bought it through Anglo-Scottish Spreading Company, one of the Lythgoe family companies. He paid £47,750 for it, reflecting the fact that property prices were on the rise.

The family, based near Warrington, was in the business of importing fertilisers from Europe and marketing them to farmers in the UK. Joseph originally intended moving to live at Collinson House himself, then changed his mind.

David and Susan Lythgoe with their first son at Collinson House.
Courtesy of David Lythgoe.

The Lythgoes' stylish automobiles parked outside. It wouldn't be the 1970s without a bright yellow boxy car! *Courtesy of David Lythgoe.*

His son David recalls: 'My father Joseph was going to move and live there then he decided not to. I got married in 1976 and the decision was taken that my wife and I would live there.

'We loved the place.

'We bought it off the Nuttalls, it was called Water's Edge then and they had it as a private house. We changed the name to Collinson House to remember the café.'

The Lythgoes carried out extensive, and much-needed, work on the property.

David says: 'We got a company to quote for painting and our architect came to have a look. He said: "Let's see what you're painting first". He stuck a penknife in one of the wooden supports and it went right through and came out the other side, so the ballroom was condemned: we had to rebuild it.'

The Lythgoes' works on the house were extensive. *Courtesy of David Lythgoe.*

Keith McArd well remembers working on this project: 'What a job! It took months to do,' he recalled.

He and his men had to cut pockets in the ballroom floor to put new girders in, horizontal and vertical, to support the whole structure.

Keith said: 'We started at one end then we worked our way around, replacing the columns either side of the window and the lintels over the window. It was rusting away.

'Obviously they'd been rendered but the render had cracked with age and it had got through to the girders and it was becoming unsafe.

'We got Wilson Collins to put the steelwork up for us, supporting the balcony, and that's a big concrete balcony – what a weight. And we were worried about it because our men were working underneath it.

'Our foreman, Brian Quirk, said to Mr Lythgoe: "Are you going to put new windows in?" And he said: "Oh no just put the old ones back" – it was taking too long, you see. I don't think it was the cost, it was to get it done quicker.

'So the columns, and the lintels too, had to be done exactly the right size to get the windows back in so it was no easy task.

'And those windows are still there, those big ones in the ballroom.'

In fact, Joseph Lythgoe didn't pay for the job anyway, as Keith went on to explain: 'What transpired after that was that [Mr Lythgoe] had employed a local firm of architects to do a survey before he bought it and he then blamed the architect for not pointing out that the rust was in these girders.

'He sued the architect's firm for the full cost of our contract so it cost him nothing – he was a tough boy!'

The *Isle of Man Examiner's* report on Joseph Lythgoe's legal action against the architects in February 1982. *Courtesy of David Lythgoe.*

The old ballroom was in particular need of restoration. *Courtesy of David Lythgoe.*

Joseph Lythgoe set up an office at Collinson House and went back to Warrington, leaving David to live there with his wife Susan and run it.

David remembered more work they did on the property, including reroofing the dome: 'The tiles all had to be numbered as they were taken off because they were all different sizes and we had to be very careful taking the gargoyles off and replacing them.'

Mark Buttery remembered working on this project: 'We restored and made the dragons on the roof 20-plus years ago. They were put on the roof to ward off evil spirits.'

David made some interesting discoveries, including initials and dates carved inside the roof by German internees and some of the original cake labels from its time as a café.

He says: 'There used to be a dumb waiter at the very top that used to go right down to the ballroom, to serve the people there. There was also an old generator between the rock and the building in case the power went off.'

Whilst he and Susan were living there he also remembers that it cost the then princely sum of £4,000 a year to heat the place.

Once the building work was completed Susan worked with an interior designer called Norma Tew on decorations and furnishings.

David was delighted with the chance to talk about their time at Collinson House, saying 'it brought back lots of happy memories'.

Their two sons, James and Johnny, were born there and the family were very much a part of the local community with David serving as treasurer for the Rushen Ambulance Service.

It's easy to imagine how magical it must have been for the young family to live in such a unique property, with its own cliffside and beach.

David said: 'The ballroom had a sprung maple floor and I was told it was one of the finest in Europe. We had a dog called Kipper and he would run towards you across the floor then sit down and slide the rest of the way.

'If you put glasses down on the cabinet on one side of the ballroom, by the time you'd walked to the other side they would have nearly fallen off!

'We planted a load of trees along the headland and we employed someone to look after the grounds and the beach.

'The sunsets and view were amazing. We used to sleep in the bedroom with the key window and we would leave that open at night and listen to the sound of the waves.'

They were especially pleased when people came and knocked on their door to tell them that they used to come to tea dances there: 'That was lovely: I even used to talk to people who'd met their husbands and wives there.'

Delightful venue for R.D.A. Cheese and Wine Party

Left to right, Mrs Jill Wood, Mr David Lythgoe, Lady Cecil, Mrs Lythgoe, Mrs Jill Gawne and Mr D. Huddleson, pictured at the R.D.A. fundraiser held at Collinson House, Port Erin, home of Mr and Mrs Lythgoe. (P)

Host Mr David Lythgoe (left) with Mrs Wendy Kirkpatrick, Mr Jack Kirkpatrick, Mrs Evelyn Haines and Mrs Jean de Vere Shortt. (P)

A LARGE crowd of supporters of Riding for the Disabled attended a Cheese and Wine evening last week at the home of Mr and Mrs D. Lythgoe, Collinson House, Spaldrick, Port Erin.

Guest of honour was group president Lady Cecil, who was accompanied by Mrs Jill Wood.

Viewing this lovely home brought back memories for many Manx guests who had known the building pre-war, when it was the very popular Collinson's Cafe and Ballroom.

and everyone agreed that despite appalling weather conditions outside, it had been a most pleasant way to raise money for such a worthwhile cause.

One gentleman and his wife pressed had held their wedding reception there on the day the Second World War broke out, and this often brought back many happy memories.

Secretary Mrs Diana Brewin [?]

Sadly, all good things come to an end and so it was for the Lythgoes.

David said: 'In 1984 I was given the choice of returning to the UK and running the family business, or staying at Collinson House and leaving the business. We were very sorry to leave. We loved the house, it was a lovely home.

'I have a lot of love and affection for the place: it was a fabulous place.'

Collinson House was perfect for entertaining. In 1982, they hosted a Cheese and Wine Evening in support of the Riding for the Disabled Association (RDA). *Courtesy of David Lythgoe.*

RIDING FOR THE DISABLED ASSOCIATION
ISLE OF MAN GROUP

Wine and Cheese Evening

at COLLINSON HOUSE, SPALDRICK, PORT ERIN
(the home of Mr. & Mrs. D. Lythgoe)

on MONDAY, 8th NOVEMBER, 1982

6.30 to 8.30 p.m.

Admission by ticket only

The Lythgoes finally left the island in 1986 and Collinson House was empty for a while. Well, not quite empty...

During this time it played host to one of the top UK bands of the 1980s.

Local resident, Mandy Karsa, recalled: 'Peter Cox and Richard Drummie from the pop band Go West moved to the island and lived for a time in Ballakillowey, just outside Port Erin.

The Go West pop stars posing on the balcony of Collinson House. *Courtesy of John Glover, Manager of Go West.*

'Their record producer, Gary Stephenson, and his wife Annette bought the Old School house nearby and I met the Go West boys and Gary at a gym in Port Erin. Gary and Annette and I became friends and still keep in touch and I've got many memories of that time.'

One of these memories is of a teen magazine organising a photoshoot of Peter and Richard and using Collinson House as the backdrop.

Mandy says: 'The magazine organised everything and set up the location and brought everybody over. They did a shot out on the balcony and another one inside in the ballroom.'

After that brief moment of fame and glamour Collinson House was about to find a new lease of life in keeping with what was also a new incarnation for the Isle of Man.

Collinson House

Port Erin, Isle of Man

This prestigious property could be your
magnificent Manx headquarters
and is now available for lease or purchase
with full planning permission for office use

Chapter Ten

Collinson House Today

After many years of local media and the public bemoaning the decline of the tourism sector on the Isle of Man, a group of prominent local businessmen and politicians, led by Sir John Bolton, had decided to do something about it.

An accountant by profession, Sir John was Chairman of the Finance Board from 1967 to 1977, effectively acting as the island's Chancellor of the Exchequer. He was realistic enough to accept that the island could no longer compete with package holidays to sunnier climes and was one of the first to spot its potential instead as an offshore finance sector.

As a self-governing entity, the Isle of Man sets its own taxes and thus could easily lower them to attract wealthy people to come and live on the island and hold assets here. This shift in policy was to lay the foundations for a period of prosperity and economic growth and a now well established financial sector that endures to this day.

As well as luring wealthy individuals with the carrot of low income tax, no stamp duty, no inheritance tax and no capital gains tax, businesses have also been attracted by the zero rate corporation tax.

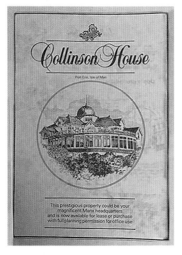

By the mid-1980s the island had really started to boom, property prices were on the rise and many banks and insurance companies were relocating or opening offices here.

The ever-canny Joseph Lythgoe had spotted this. When he put Collinson House up for sale he decided that marketing it as a commercial property might bring a better price.

Beneath the heading Collinson House and a pen-and-ink drawing, the front page of the sales brochure read: 'This prestigious property could be your magnificent Manx headquarters and is now available for lease or purchase with full planning permission for office use.'

The sales brochure for Collinson House emphasised its potential as a commercial space. *Courtesy of David Lythgoe.*

Isle of Man Examiner, Friday, 10th August, 1984

New restaurant and shopping complex

AFTER a number of years as a private residence Collinson House, at Spaldrick, Port Erin, is to be restored to its former glories as a restaurant and shopping complex.

Potential tenants in the Island have been sent a brochure by Mr Joseph Lythgoe, of Gartshores Ltd., Swinhoe House, Culcheth, Warrington, who bought the property in 1974.

He recalls that it was built by the Collinson family as a prestige restaurant and holiday complex in the early part of the century and that many people in Port Erin "still recall with pleasure the dinner dances of the 1930's."

RESTORED

Over the last 10 years the building has been restored to high standards and Mr Lythgoe's son David and his family have lived there. But they are leaving the

(cont. on p. 4)

The *Isle of Man Examiner* reported on Joseph Lythgoe's efforts to sell the house in August 1984.

Inside were listed the property's key features: an upper ground floor which included the bedroom with the distinctive 'key-shaped' window where David and Susan Lythgoe had slept and which gave access to the 2,000 sq ft balcony; the turret room above with another bedroom, and the lower ground floor with the 2,000 sq ft ballroom and a large fitted kitchen and larder.

The wording went on to suggest that, although planning permission had been given for the whole property to be used as office accommodation, there was also the option to use part of the upper floor as living accommodation.

In 1982 Joseph Lythgoe had transferred ownership of the property from the Anglo-Scottish Spreading Company into another family company, Adam Lythgoe (Agriculture) Limited (later known as 'Gartshores') for the sum of £130,000. He plainly had no wish to incur agent's fees in any future sale and put his own name on the brochure for any enquiries. A local caretaker was available to open the property for anyone wishing to view it.

Sheila Bailey had come to live on the Isle of Man when her husband Neville was appointed Chief Medical Officer.

Sheila had been awarded a Churchill Fellowship in the creation of small businesses, something she says she is passionate about. She had an office in St George's Street, in Douglas, offering 'all the support you felt small businesses needed' and when she saw Collinson House in 1986 it appeared to offer an ideal opportunity to expand this enterprise.

Sheila says: 'I wanted to run courses specifically for women in business and it was a beautiful building.

'Joseph Lythgoe was doing the negotiation himself and he really admired what I was doing and he sold it to me for what I felt was a very reasonable price.'

It was indeed a 'reasonable price': just £130,000, which the company had valued it at for the books four years previously. It may even have been that Joseph at this point just wanted to move on because Gartshores even loaned the Baileys £30,000 against the property to facilitate the purchase.

Sheila and Neville had recently sold their own property and had their eye on another one which was about to come onto the market so they were also able to use Collinson House as their home.

'It had a very nice kitchen and all sorts of things,' she says.

When it came to the courses she was running, the ballroom was used. Sheila brought over the head of a major women's training company in Europe and hired a camera so that the participants could practise talking into a camera and making presentations.

But the Baileys did not stay for long: having purchased Collinson House in December 1986 they sold it again in 1987 to life assurance company, NEL Britannia. It turned out to be a very nice little earner for the Baileys: the price they got for it was £220,000.

Sheila says: 'Their chairman, Viscount Gort, wanted to make it into very luxurious offices.

'He commissioned his wife, Lady Gort, who was a well-known interior designer, to realise his ideas.

'It was such an amazing place and it was such an opportunity for us to be there. It deserves to be celebrated.'

Doing Business in Style

COLLINSON HOUSE
the new headquarters of
NEL Britannia International Assurance Ltd. (Isle of Man)

In Port Erin, you could not miss Collinson House if you tried: the white stone rotunda, towering high above Port Erin beach, half-way up the steep gradient of Spaldrick Road, may be seen from almost every part of town. As a landmark, it stands up to its immediate vis-a-vis, Milner Tower and, at the close of the day, when the sunset flashes back from the enormous picture windows, it becomes a blazing beacon.

The three-storied structure, designed in the Chinese style popular in the Edwardian era, was erected in 1913 by a Quaker family from Halifax, the Collinsons. Originally merchant tea firms in alcoholic beverages, they seem to have suffered from qualms of conscience about the nature of their activities, to the extent of transferring all their brewery interests into the importation of tea, coffee and cocoa.

Collinson House, fondly remembered locally as 'the old dance hall', was intended from the start as a 'tea-house' where, every afternoon, a smartly

Collinson House, Port Erin

dressed clientele would indulge in such decorous pastimes as tea-drinking and tango to the subdued strains of a Palm Court orchestra. A world war came and went, the charleston succeeded the tango, and still crowds glided on over the polished oak floors, between sips of the best Darjeeling and thin cucumber sandwiches. It was not until the early forties, when all hell broke loose, leaving no corner of Europe undisturbed, that the tea-rooms had to make way for an internment camp, an event recently recorded in the BBC 2 programme which won the prize for the best short film on television.

Thereafter, Collinson House's fortunes followed the Island's own. It was demoted to Collinson Cafe when Manx tourism went downmarket in the early fifties, enjoyed a brief spell as a private house during the boom years and, in 1976, was finally granted its current status as a building for mixed office and

residential use, thanks to the vision of an influential industrialist, Mr. Joseph Lithgoe, who was quick to realise its potential both as a home and as a base for his extensive company network.

Mr. Lithgoe did much more than just change the use of the place. A dedicated conservationist, he spent some £250,000 restoring it, down to the minutest architectural detail, as well as replanting the neglected grounds with a number of fine trees and bushes. When he went back to the mainland a few years later, Collinson House was alive again, and a further - and transient - conversion into a restaurant, in 1984, left no scars.

From then on, its destinies took an upturn. The next owner, Mrs. Sheila Bailey, founder of the successful Enterprise Training and Development project and a socially-aware businesswoman, planned to turn the building

Grand entrance to the new NEL Britannia offices

Reprinted from Manx Life, November 1987

Doing Business in Style

Director Viscount Gort and General Manager Colette Henerty

into a management training centre, but was soon forced to acknowledge that, although the dimensions of the public rooms were ideal for those purposes, the lack [of] accommodation would not be suitable. As a result, the alternative, it was too big for two ... to discover a ... who would fit the code.

She had come to International ... Young Professional Year panel, who ... thirty year old Colette Henerty ... caring, welfare function. As it happened, having to move premises, due ... After consulting ... gave his wholehearted ... Collinson House ... Bailey agreed to ... hands. The ... live on.

The relationship ... fice and the young ... riage between ... promises to be ... business, like the ... January 1985, a ... concern enabling ... from the tax-exempt status of the funds held by a U.K.-based multinational, Britannia Arrow Holdings PLC, NEL Britannia International Assurance Ltd.

(Isle of Man) has grown from two to twenty-seven staff in less than three years. As for the parent group, which specialises in long-term assurance and fund management, with associated merchant banking and unit trust operation, it was recently valued in excess of £500 million on the London Stock Exchange. "We deal solely with British expatriates and international investors", explains Miss Henerty, "so there was no real need for us to be in Douglas. Not only is the property a splendid investment in itself, but it has every added advantage of situation, size, and proximity to the airport. And the long and short of it is that we fell in love at first sight !"

That they did is obvious from the care that has been taken in the decoration - a mellow combination of lavender, gold, russet, and moss, echoing the shades of the surrounding cliffs and masterminded by Lady Gort, wife of Viscount Gort, one of the eleven members of a Board which also includes the Earl of

The former ballroom, now the main office

Northesk. Chintz curtains drape the windows, a honey-coloured carpet covers both the floors and the noble staircase, heavy crystal chandeliers hang from all the ceilings, and landscapes by local artists are displayed in

Royal Skandia (NEL Britannia) was certainly "doing business in style" from Collinson House, as this news feature makes clear. *Courtesy of Manx Life*

The new island HQ for NEL Britannia, which became Royal Skandia soon afterwards, opened in the late summer of 1987 with Colette Henerty in charge.

In December Anne Clucas joined the company. She recalled: 'The business had moved from Athol Street in Douglas to Collinsons. I worked in the personal portfolio department as an administrator.

'There were no computers in those days: we used ledgers and they used to bounce up and down on the desk whenever someone crossed the floor.

'There was one computer up in the dome. This produced clients' valuations every quarter and there was one member of staff based up there by herself: it was her domain.'

Because they were slightly out of the village in Port Erin and all the shops in the row nearby had long closed down, a woman was employed to walk up to Collinson House each day and serve lunches for them in the kitchen, usually sandwiches or pasta.

Debbie Stephens who also worked there adds: 'We had food delivered for lunch every day by the International Hotel School which was in one of the old hotels on the hill. We ate very well while working there! And we had a lady who came in to serve us the lunch too. She was wonderful. Can't remember her name but such a lovely lady.'

This sense of isolation also led to great camaraderie among the 26-strong workforce. Anne said: 'Because it was so small we all became really good friends and they were very happy days.

'It was a beautiful place to work, except in the winter: the stormy seas were quite spectacular but a bit scary.

'I have lovely memories, it was very enjoyable.'

In line with most other financial institutions on the island at that time, Royal Skandia experienced rapid growth. And, glamorous as it might have been, the truth was that Collinson House was not ideally suited to being office accommodation: the novelty of bouncy floors and offices in turrets tends to wear off quite quickly when you have work to get done.

By 1995 the company was looking to move to larger premises in Douglas where all the action was in the island's financial sector so Collinson House was once again put up for sale.

And along came a certain Mr James Mellon, more generally known as 'Jim'.

Fresh from building a significant fortune in Asia and Russia, in 1994 Jim had started establishing a business base on the Isle of Man. He already had a home in Ibiza and he was assembling a sizeable portfolio of rental property in Germany.

He has said that he finds buying property irresistible: 'I have to get people to hold me back,' he says.

Imagine, then, the lure of a property like Collinson House for Jim: its sheer uniqueness and the possibilities it presented.

When it came to fulfilling his vision for the property, Keith McArd and his team were once again called in, along with Jim's then-property manager and a structural engineer, John Gray.

Collinson House during Jim's recent renovation. *Courtesy of Ben Humbles.*

What Jim had in mind was no small ask, given the nature of the site, which Keith already knew well.

He recalled: 'The present owner, Mr Mellon, when he bought it he wanted it all dug out for more rooms underneath.

'We started the work for him, digging out underneath the [ballroom] floor, to form another floor. Underneath the big windows there was a wall and there were big buttresses to hold the wall up because it's on a really steep slope.

'In between those buttresses Mr Mellon wanted windows putting in so we put in the framework for the glass. To get that soil dug out and then lifted out onto a lorry was no mean task, on that steep hill. We were coming up with a digger and digging just a scoop at a time, coming up the slope and putting it into the lorry to cart away.'

Sadly, the building work meant that the ballroom's celebrated sprung floor became a casualty, although the beautiful maple timbers have been retained and relaid. And, for all its size, this room with its wall of glass looking out to sea, is surprisingly cosy and relaxed. (Although this of course could be partly down to the frequent sight of dogs sprawling happily on the settees!)

The ballroom has lost its sprung dance floor, but the maple timbers have been retained. *Courtesy of Lincoln Forrest.*

Jim stays at Collinson House when he can: he has spent several Christmases there.

And, ironically for someone known for his peripatetic lifestyle, Jim found himself spending several months in lockdown at Collinson House during the Covid-19 pandemic. It was springtime and it coincided with a long spell of glorious weather so Jim and his partner Dafina had the opportunity to enjoy the house to the full and experience what it must have been like to spend time there in those long ago times when Port Erin was thronged with tourists and Collinson's Café was the place to be.

No one saw the end coming for those golden days. Certainly Ted Collinson, when he built the property, could not have imagined it being used by wartime internees any more than he could have imagined it as the offices of a global life assurance company.

Jim's dogs at Collinson.
Courtesy of Dafina Grapci.

As Professor Hugh Davidson, chairman of the Rushen Heritage Trust, points out: 'It is highly unusual for the same building, without much reconstruction and with the essential elements of the original building intact, to have been successfully used for four very different purposes.'

One thing the past tells us is how hard the future is to predict but you certainly wouldn't bet against more twists of fate bringing yet another incarnation for this extraordinary property.

The house may have changed, but the vista has not. Jim's guests at Collinson House, like previous generations of visitors, enjoy the fine view over Spaldrick Bay.

Christmas at Collinson.

Collinson House

COLLINSON'S CAFÉ
PORT ERIN
ISLE OF MAN

Then

and now

Collinson House

The View from the Dome